BOWOOD REVISITED

Bowood staff reception, summer 2016
© Hallmark Photography, Calne

BOWOOD REVISITED:
The revival of a country estate

Kate Fielden

ELSP

Published in 2016 by
ELSP
in association with the Bowood Estate

Origination by Ex Libris Press
www.ex-librisbooks.co.uk

Printed by CPI Anthony Rowe
Chippenham, Wiltshire

ISBN 978-1-906641-99-3

Image acknowledgements are given where the
photographer is known; uncredited images share
Bowood Estate copyright or, if copyright is at
present unknown, an apology is given.

*Cover photograph: Bowood House from
the lake by Anna Stowe, October 2015*

CONTENTS

The Marquis and Marchioness of Lansdowne, 2016

Foreword by Lord Lansdowne

Memories are short and with the effluxion of time, dates become confused. When did we do that? What year did we open to the public? When did we start building the adventure playground? When did we establish the soft fruit business and when did it stop and why? All these and a thousand more memories flood through the mind and unless they are chronologically anchored they become blurred. Change is not only inevitable but necessary, otherwise enterprises ossify and die. The pace of change over the past forty four years has, however, been so dramatic that I felt it was important to record the evolution of Bowood since I became custodian in 1972.

Kate Fielden, former Bowood Curator, and I have met over several recorded interviews so that we might put together an account to include my own recollections, along with additional facts and dates garnered from the Estate records. This short history, no more than a blink of the eye in the story of this special place, is the combined outcome of those memories and researches. It happily coincides with celebration of just over forty years of opening Bowood to the public.

Our continuing success is due, in very large part, not only to the constant support and active participation of my wife but also thanks to past and present staff, too many for all to be mentioned, whose loyalty and expertise have been paramount.

It gives us enormous pleasure to share this historic oasis of Bowood with our tens of thousands of visitors each year and I very much hope that this account will be enjoyed by those to whom it may be of interest.

Charlie Lansdowne,

The Marquis of Lansdowne

Introduction

Bowood was first opened to the public just over forty years ago, in 1975. This short publication has been produced to celebrate that event. It gives a brief history of Bowood and a more detailed, chronological account of the 9th Marquis of Lansdowne's stewardship from 1972 to the present day.

The tale is a fascinating one, for it chronicles the evolution and successful continuation of a landed estate with its associated local communities and workforce over a period which has seen great changes. These changes have occurred not only in the management of the English countryside and the care of historic properties but also in the extraordinary revolution brought about by the rapid development of information technology. The enormous expansion and immediacy of global influences has made the world a much smaller place than it seemed to be only 25 years ago, enabling individuals and organizations to reach out to it in ways hitherto unimaginable. It was critical to Bowood's survival to move forward, trying always to keep abreast of these events and not to resist them.

There were, however, serious doubts about Bowood's future following the Second World War and demolition of the 'Big House'. These uncertainties were compounded by difficulties experienced by many owners of our great country houses at that time who suffered severe financial restraints, some of which were the outcome of an adverse political climate and crippling taxation. Later on, landowners who were not crushed by earlier constraints were hit by the decline of agriculture in the 1980s. Even today, the increasing burden of taxation on landed estates is a critical factor as to whether or not they will survive.

Bowood House is still lived in by the family whose ancestors purchased the estate in 1754. That Bowood has continued to exist, following the deprivations and financial setbacks arising from the last war, is due in large measure to the dedication of its present owner, The Marquis of Lansdowne, who took over from his father in 1972 at the age of 31. The then Lord Shelburne, with the confidence and enthusiasm of youth, and faith in the value of preserving and cherishing something exceptional in its own right, has not only succeeded in keeping Bowood alive and flourishing into the 21st century but also in nurturing it as a unique resource, hugely appreciated for its beauty and tranquillity by its many visitors from all over the world as well as those who live nearby and have contributed to its success.

The Bowood Estate today comprises a Grade I Listed 18th-century country house and garden, with adjacent pleasure grounds, set in about 1,500 acres of similarly Listed parkland which remains substantially a late 18th-century designed landscape by 'Capability' Brown. There are some 700 acres of managed woodland and 500 acres of land farmed in hand, some of it within the park. Beyond the formal park are around 1,800 acres of farmland let out to local farmers.

Bowood House and terraces today

At the heart of the estate is Bowood House, a Georgian mansion with a 4-acre walled garden and its adjoining buildings mainly associated with grounds and garden maninenance activities. Former service buildings close by the house have been converted to estate offices.

The house and gardens are open to the public from Easter until early November. For the convenience of visitors and ease of access, some former garden buildings have been brought into different uses and new facilities have been constructed.

The Osprey yard complex, some distance to the northwest of the house, developed in the early 19th century as workshops and storage units for maintenance of the estate and its buildings, is still used for this purpose. Alongside The Osprey are the working estate timber yard and the golf course machinery maintenance workshop and garage.

To the west of the house, in an area of former farmland lying within Brown's park, is now located an 18-hole championship golf course with clubhouse and restaurant, associated hospitality and conference rooms, and a 43-bed luxury hotel. The four-bed Queenwood Golf Lodge, a 19th-century *cottage ornée* built on the site of an earlier farmstead, nestles in the centre of the golf course. The whole complex, constructed within the last 25 years and partly incorporating the Listed Home Farm House and barns, is known as the Bowood Hotel, Spa & Golf Resort.

The Bowood Estate does not exist in isolation. The nearby village of Derry Hill and Studley, on the northern fringe of the park and close to the main 'Golden Gates' park entrance was the principal estate village up until the mid 20th century, most of the houses having been built, maintained and let by the Estate for its employees to live in. Though many of these older houses are now privately owned, others still belong to and are let by the Estate, including those lived in by current and retired Bowood employees. Newer houses have been constructed on former estate land where road and place names have Bowood associations. Strong Bowood links are also seen in fine public buildings, such as the church, school, village hall and pub: all built from the 19th century onwards wholly or in part by the Lansdownes. Now with over 1,200 inhabitants, Derry Hill and Studley has grown from a small linear settlement on the edge of the park to be the largest village in Calne Without Parish.

Sandy Lane, on the western edge of the park, is a former Bowood Estate village. Some of its cottages may have been built in the 1760s to house inhabitants of Mannings Hill hamlet, relocated to make way for the Bowood lake. The cottages were rebuilt in the mid 19th century in the 'Old English' style also seen at Derry Hill; most of them are now privately owned. Attractive lodges in the same architectural style remain standing at entrances or former entrances to the park.

Bowood has a long association with the nearby town of Calne. In the past, the Lansdownes owned much property here, including a number of businesses; they effectively appointed their own men (including some family members) as Liberal MPs for the borough, and almost to the present day have been closely involved in its local governance. Again, the town has enjoyed generous Lansdowne benefactions and retains numerous family connections in its buildings, schools and street names.

The links between Bowood and the people who live in the nearby communities are vital and beneficial to both. This may, perhaps, have been more so in the past when interdependence was greater, but it remains so at the present time – for it is largely local people who are employed at Bowood and help to supply many of its needs, regularly enjoying what Bowood offers in return.

The writer is indebted to Lord Lansdowne for fundamental discussions at each stage of this account. More information was obtained from the Bowood archives, notably from the annual reports to the Bowood Trustees. Many former and present Bowood staff members have also given helpful advice and information.

Chapter one

Bowood before 1972

The Bowood Estate, formerly part of the Royal Forest of Pewsham, was purchased in 1754 by Anglo-Irishman John Petty Fitzmaurice, 1st Earl of Shelburne (1705–1761). He had previously bought the manor of nearby Bremhill and was developing holdings in Wiltshire with a fortune inherited from his uncle in 1751. Work began almost immediately on improving the early Georgian house and gardens at Bowood and by the time of his death, in 1761, two extensive E-shaped office courts, designed by architect Henry Keene, as well as a large walled garden had been completed.

The 1st Earl's widow commissioned the Adam Brothers to build a mausoleum for him in the park, while his son William, the 2nd Earl and later 1st Marquess (1737–1805), employed the same architects to redesign the principal rooms within the house (subsequently known as the Big House) and behind it a grand orangery wing, completed c.1768, to front the two office courts (the Little House). During the 1770s the two parts of Bowood House were joined together by a large drawing room after a design by Robert Adam.

1st Marquess of Lansdowne, portrait in oils by J.-L. Mosnier, c.1780 (detail)

Bowood from the lake, engraving, c.1800

While building works were taking place in the 1760s, the park was enlarged and altered, including formation of the lake, to a plan by leading landscape architect 'Capability' Brown. In 1765, Shelburne (later Lansdowne) House, in London, built by the Adam Brothers, was purchased and then furnished in grand style. Over the same period, the estate was greatly enlarged, with purchases of property in Calne as well as extensive areas of farmland southwards to the Marlborough Downs.

The 2nd Earl, who spent most of his life in politics, was Prime Minister briefly from 1782 to 1783. Having negotiated peace with America, he was created Marquess of Lansdowne in 1784. During his retirement from government in the 1780s, and with the advice of the Hon. Charles Hamilton of Painshill, he ordered the construction of a rockwork valley and cascade in the 'Picturesque' style, below Brown's dam at the head of the lake.

All of these works demanded the employment of a large number of local people, most of whom were housed in estate cottages within or on the edge of the park. Those who worked in the house and lived nearby were known as 'The Family' and their very close association with the Lansdownes always gave them a special place in the running of the household. A small school was set up for impoverished children who were fed and clothed at the Estate's expense; while what might now be termed welfare payments were made to those unfit to work for reasons of age or infirmity.

The cascade at Bowood (Anna Stowe, 2016)

Quite apart from his land purchases and building and garden-construction projects, the 1st Marquess amassed collections of furniture and works of art that were famous in his own time, notably his paintings and Classical sculpture.

Although the 1st Marquess' stewardship can be seen as the first great period of growth and prosperity at Bowood, this came to an end on his death in 1805 when it was revealed that he had hugely overspent on embellishing his houses and gardens and his estate was bankrupt. His son, the 2nd Marquess, did not return to Bowood, for its contents, garden furniture and finest timber had all been sold to pay his father's debts; his properties, including Bowood, were heavily mortgaged.

In 1809, the 2nd Marquess was succeeded by his half-brother Henry who, like his father, was to become a leading Whig statesman and patron of the arts. Chancellor of the Exchequer in 1806 at the age of 25, he served under eight prime ministers and was three times Lord President of the Council. In 1818 he succeeded to the title and was the beneficiary of his cousin, the Earl of Kerry, and it is assumed that he was able to restore Bowood and Lansdowne House at least in part with Lord Kerry's legacy. Bowood prospered once again under a second great period of building and garden

3rd Marquess of Lansdowne, portrait in oils by T. Lawrence, c.1820 (detail)

design. A number of the principal rooms in the house were redecorated by Sir Charles Barry and Charles Cockerell in the Neo Classical style, the latter being responsible for redesigning the Adam library and creating the chapel between the two courts of the Little House. The clock tower over the chapel was rebuilt by Sir Charles Barry. The great Italianate terraces, the upper by Robert Smirke and the lower, by George Kennedy, were constructed in front of the orangery wing in 1818 and 1851, respectively; while the rhododendron gardens were established around the mausoleum. In the 1840s a pinetum and an arboretum were begun in the pleasure grounds behind the walled garden.

It was at this time that the estate villages of Derry Hill and Sandy Lane were rebuilt in the 'Old English' style, and a number of community buildings, such as the church, non-conformist chapels and school were constructed there – as were the fine lodges at gates to the park, including the splendid Italianate 'Golden Gates' main entrance in Derry Hill, designed by Sir Charles Barry, c.1845. With good management and adequate finance, Bowood was once again the largely self-sufficient organization it had been under the 1st Marquess during the 1760s and 1770s, relying almost entirely upon its workforce and own produce to maintain itself and supply Lansdowne House in London. The Estate ran its own brickworks and stone quarry, undertook all its building, maintenance and repair work, managed its farms and woodlands, and made use of the new canal and railway network to bring manufactured and other goods to and from Bowood.

Bowood House and Terraces, watercolour by G. Kennedy, 1851
(Jarrold & Sons Ltd.)

The 3rd Marquess died in 1863 and over the following 60 years the family's fortunes gradually declined under the 4th, 5th and 6th Marquesses. The 4th Marquess did not long survive his father and was succeeded by his son Henry in 1866.

The 5th Marquess (1845–1927), determined to restore some order, straight away commissioned a complete survey of the Bowood Estate, mapping and listing all the land holdings, properties and farms that he had inherited. Cottages were renovated, and some 300 new dwellings were constructed in his time. It became apparent, however, that his extensive estates in England, Scotland and Ireland were no longer profitable owing to low or non-existent rental income and he was obliged to take important offices abroad in order to retain them. Even so, as Governor-General of Canada (1883–88) and Viceroy of India (1888–94), he kept very close contact with Bowood through regular correspondence with his Agents John Spencer and Henry Herbert Smith. He sent seeds and young trees from abroad to be raised in the park and pleasure grounds and kept abreast of the latest farming methods via journals and newspapers. On his return to England, in addition to his full-time duties of state, he rationalized the running of the Bowood Estate and gardens, cutting down on the glass housing as well as the workforce in order to reduce expenditure. Electricity was installed in the house, and the kitchens and offices were reorganised on a more practical scale. He continued to plant new trees and shrubs and, by our standards and without full-scale mechanization, his workforce remained comparatively large.

Within a few years, however, that workforce was further reduced at the onset of the First World War. The orangery was turned into a military hospital, flowerbeds into vegetable plots; and substantial amounts of timber, game and other produce were requisitioned for the war effort. The Estate was never to recover fully from this rapid change in circumstances and emphasis: no longer self-sufficient, it was now required, with reduced manpower, to support a larger enterprise that did not return a profit. The outcome was inevitable: estate buildings were not properly maintained, the woodlands were neglected and only urgent priorities were attended to. Immediate cash was raised from time to time by selling pictures and other important works of art.

The 5th Marquess died in 1927. So close was his relationship with the villagers who supported Bowood through difficult times with their loyalty, service and skills, that he chose to be buried in the churchyard at Derry Hill, rather than in the family mausoleum in the park; his wife was later buried beside him. His younger son, Charles, to whom he had handed over his mother's Perthshire estate in 1914, had been killed in action at Ypres in October that year. His elder son, Henry (1872–1936), took on what must by then have been the considerable burden of running Bowood. Since his father's time, the Big House, expensive to heat, maintain and repair, had been used only for large events and house parties, the family living more comfortably in the east wing of the Little House.

5th Marquess of Lansdowne, portrait in oils by P. De Laszlo, 1920
(Jarrold & Sons Ltd.)

Lansdowne House, hitherto a substantial drain on financial resources, was sold in 1929. The estate was run more or less on a shoestring and things did not improve in the years leading up to the Second World War.

The 7th Marquess, Charles (1917–1944), succeeded his father at the age of 20. Three years later he was a serving soldier, having left the running of the estate in the hands of his mother and Bowood Agent Oscar Hood. His younger brother Edward (Ned) joined up as soon as he could. Both young men were killed in action in 1944: Ned in Normandy, and Charles in Italy not long afterwards, on 20 August. This terrible tragedy for the Lansdowne family was to herald very significant changes.

The Marquessate and Bowood passed to Major George Mercer Nairne, cousin of the 7th Marquess and son of Lord Charles Mercer Nairne killed at Ypres in 1914. At the time of the 7th Marquess' death, Major Mercer Nairne was taking part in the Normandy Invasion, having been seconded from the Royal Scots Greys to fight with the Free French under General Leclerc, first in North Africa and then as a liaison officer with the Resistance in France. At that time, the Big House at Bowood was occupied by Westonbirt School for Girls, evacuated by the military from their school premises in Gloucestershire. The 6th Lord Lansdowne's widow, who married Lord Colum Crichton-Stuart in 1940, her elder daughter Lady Katherine (Kitty) Bigham with her young family, and her younger daughter Elizabeth were all living in the Little House. Lady Elizabeth attended Westonbirt School in the Big House. Lady Colum, struggling to keep Bowood going under wartime restrictions, was not informed officially of her son Lord Lansdowne's death until December 1944. By this time, Major Mercer Nairne had taken part in the liberation of Paris (25 August 1944), and was now employed as Private Secretary to Sir Alfred Duff Cooper, British Ambassador to France. It was with some reluctance that he took up his hitherto wholly unexpected – and what must have been to some extent unwelcome – duties as 8th Marquis of Lansdowne.

The 8th Marquis (1912–1999), who preferred, as does the present Marquis, to use the French spelling, had been brought up partly at Meikleour, his father's home in Perthshire, and partly in London and Kent, following his widowed mother's remarriage to John Jacob, 1st Baron Astor of Hever. In 1938 he married Barbara, only daughter of wealthy American businessman Harold Chase. When he succeeded to the Lansdowne title, they had two young children: Caroline, born in 1939 and Charles, born in 1941, and their family home

8th Marquis of Lansdowne, portrait in oils by Norman Hepple, 1979
(Jarrold & Sons Ltd.)

was Meikleour. The war had already altered their circumstances, for on her husband's enlisting, Barbara had moved to America to work in the British Embassy's press office in Washington where her task, as the wife of a British serving officer, was to help to encourage the United States to enter the war on the Allies' side. Her daughter Caroline stayed with her grandparents in Santa Barbara, California, where her son Charles was born: both children were cared for by a young Scottish nanny, Jean Patterson, while their mother was in Washington. Early in 1944, Barbara Mercer Nairne and her two children returned to Meikleour which was then being used as a maternity hospital.

By December 1944, with the official announcement of the 7th Marquess' death, the new Lord and Lady Lansdowne were faced with the enormous problem of how to reorganise their lives. They visited Bowood, where Lady Kitty and her husband Edward Bigham were living in the Little House. Westonbirt School had returned to Gloucestershire in 1944 and the Big House was now let until 1945 to the Air Ministry as a hostel for VIPs flying in and out of nearby Lyneham. The Home Farm was just surviving on a skeleton staff while the unploughed parts of the park and the pleasure grounds were cut for hay. The walled garden and the woodlands had been seriously neglected.

The Lansdownes decided at first to use Buckhill House, formerly the Bowood Agent's home on the northern edge of the estate, as their base. The Bighams remained as tenants in the Little House, giving the family some time to sort out the very complicated situation that had arisen concerning inheritance.

The 5th Marquess, under the Settled Land Act (1925) had ensured that his land holdings would pass to his successors but there were restrictions on re-sale or profitable leasing of the land, resulting in potential difficulties in realizing any value from it – especially critical at the end of the war when land prices had reached rock bottom. Thus, although Bowood passed into the 8th Marquis' ownership, little capital could be gained from it when large amounts of hard cash were badly needed to put the estate and its many buildings back into good order. The situation was further complicated since, apart from a number of yet to be specified 'Heirlooms' to be left in Trust to his successor, the 7th Marquess had bequeathed the remainder of his possessions, including the contents of Bowood, to his sisters. Lady Kitty, his elder sister, and her husband Edward (later Lord Mersey), as Trustees of the Will, decided which items should be designated as Heirlooms, to be placed alongside the house and pleasure grounds in a Will Trust. The 'Heirlooms' comprised family portraits and other treasures that it was felt should stay at Bowood because of their historic family connections. These were possessions which, even if of some value, could not be sold. Thus it was at this time that the last major dispersal of the once-famous Lansdowne Collection of paintings and other works of art took place, as unencumbered family possessions were either sold to pay death duties or distributed amongst the 7th Marquess' immediate family members.

Largely owing to the generosity of Lady Kitty, however, many of the contents of Bowood, including fine pieces of furniture and paintings, were given to the 8th Marquis so that the house might remain furnished. In return, Lord Lansdowne gave Derreen, his Irish estate near Kenmare in County Kerry, to the Bighams.

The Bighams remained as tenants at Bowood until 1951. The Lansdownes and their growing family – now including Robert, born in 1947 and Georgina, in 1950, were rarely at Bowood, mainly dividing their time between Meikleour and their London flat. They usually came down to Wiltshire at Easter, and again in the autumn for the hunting season. They were well cared for at Buckhill House by housekeeper Florence Townsend and her husband, Frank, who acted as driver and also looked after the horses. In 1947, Lord Lansdowne legally included the Lansdowne family name of Petty-Fitzmaurice in his own surname.

Curiously, given the difficulties that ownership of Bowood posed for him, Lord Lansdowne did not take the easy option and simply sell up: it was, perhaps, primarily a sense of duty that persuaded him to try to make something of it. During the early post-war years, he was not alone in owning a great country house and sizeable estate that could neither make a profit nor break even. Unearned Income Tax on investments rose to 98 per cent in 1950 and it seemed likely that land nationalization might be imposed, along with the nationalization of coal, steel, and the railways that had already taken place. The Bowood Estate was semi-derelict, including the Big House, the farms, and many of the estate buildings and cottages.

Bowood House and Gardens, aerial view, 1934, showing the Big House before demolition in 1955 (Historic England Archive)

Following the election of a Conservative Government in 1951, those responsible for land management hoped for some improvement in their circumstances. Nevertheless, the situation for many landed estates still looked hopeless. The highest number so far of England's great houses was demolished in the 1950s, often by impecunious owners who could not afford to keep them standing: the Big House at Bowood was among them. Slowly falling into serious disrepair and not fit to live in, it would have required very considerable sums to put the house in order. Plans were drawn up for its possible conversion to a school and thought was given to turning it into a hotel. Finally, in 1954, despairing of a practical and economically viable solution for its future, Lord Lansdowne decided upon demolition and the task was undertaken by local contractor Peter White in 1955, following a sale of architectural fixtures and fittings.

After the Bighams had left the Big House, the Lansdownes, when in Wiltshire, stayed in the Little House, more or less camping in the nursery wing on the first floor, until improvements designed by architect

Frederick Sortain Samuels had been completed in the late 1950s. Their real home during this time remained at Meikleour.

The funds to undertake the necessary improvements to the house and to begin to bring the Bowood Estate back into order were raised by selling Wiltshire properties and farmland that were sadly of little value at that time, often being compromised by fixed life tenancies. In 1954, one thousand five hundred acres of tenanted farmland were sold in the Calstone area for just over £17 an acre. It was depressing to find that land sold to tenants could be re-sold unencumbered for more than twice as much. In all, around 5,000 acres of land were sold by the 8th Marquis. From time to time, throughout the fifties and sixties, it was also found necessary to sell pictures and other works of art as well, in order to keep the Estate going. Concerned about the cost of repairs, in 1951 Lord Lansdowne offered 25 cottages in the estate village of Sandy Lane to the National Trust which refused them for lack of financial endowment.

From 1957 to 1958 the 8th Marquis held the office of Lord-in-Waiting. He was then employed in Government as Joint Parliamentary Under-Secretary of State in the Foreign Office (1958–62). While working for the Foreign Office he narrowly avoided travelling in a plane that crashed in Northern Rhodesia, killing UN Secretary General Dag Hammarskjold on 18 September 1961. He became Minister of State for Commonwealth and Colonial Affairs (1962–64) and was appointed a Privy Councillor in 1964.

During those post-war years the Estate Office at Bowood was largely run day-to-day by Ted Holman who had worked under earlier Bowood agents from the time of the 6th Marquess, providing an important element of continuity between the old and new regimes. Under the 8th Marquis, the range of buildings in Top Yard, which formerly included the electricity generator for the house, was converted to estate offices.

The Home and Pinhills Farms were brought back in hand and run with small Ayrshire dairy herds, each of about 100 cows. The woodland was put under the supervision of trained Head Forester George Harrison, while the walled garden was temporarily let as a market garden. A tennis court and swimming pool were constructed in one of the walled garden quarters in 1956–57. Slowly, Bowood began to awake from a lengthy slumber, but the losses through sales necessary to achieve that awakening continued to reduce the estate considerably in size. Further finance was obtained by selling some land for building, including that at Derry Hill which allowed the first phased expansion of the village with modern houses in the mid sixties.

By the early 1970s, Lord Lansdowne, who had married again in 1969 following the death in 1965 of his first wife, had begun to think about retirement to Meikleour and the possibility of asking Lord Shelburne to take Bowood on in his place.

Chapter two

Lord Shelburne's early life

Lord Shelburne was born Charles Maurice Mercer Nairne, in Santa Barbara, California, on 21st February 1941 where he lived with his grandparents and elder sister Caroline until the age of three. In 1944, he and his sister, accompanied by their nanny, took a train to New Orleans and left America on a hazardous wartime journey across the Atlantic in a Portuguese ship to Lisbon. From there they found seats on an aeroplane to Prestwick and eventually reached their home in Scotland to join their mother who had flown direct from Washington. It was later that year that the Mercer Nairnes were to learn of the extraordinary change in their circumstances.

From that time, the growing family lived mostly at Meikleour which they always thought of as home. Family visits were made to Bowood at Easter but summer holidays were often spent in Ireland. Lord Shelburne remembers little of Bowood as a boy and recalls his first summer day there as an 11-year-old on an outing from Spyway school, arriving with his joint headmasters, both driving Lagondas with four pupils each as passengers. They picnicked on Lake Field and the young boy was deeply impressed by the vivid green of the grass and tall rushes by the water – and the extraordinary sight of the huge, empty house on the skyline.

At Meikleour the Lansdowne children had school and other local friends to play with and later on, when shooting and fishing were the main boyhood passions, Scotland seemed to be very much the best place to be. Holidays at Bowood were usually without friends of one's own age but Charlie and his elder sister enjoyed playing in the derelict Big House and the excitement of exploring its roofs. The imposing front hall, used as a grain store in the early fifties, was heaped with corn which added its dusty aroma to the sweet smell of dry rot. They spent much time with Frank and Mrs Townsend, who lived permanently close by at Rose Cottage and between them looked after the house and the horses. They also enjoyed chatting below stairs with chef Jo MacLennan and Percy Hitchcock, the butler who travelled with the family to and from Meikleour.

8th Marquis of Lansdowne and family, Meikleour, 1947

The Big House at Bowood under demolition, 1955 (Peter White)

After the Big House had gone, improvements to the Little House made it much more comfortable to live in. The children were away at school during term time: Lord Shelburne started at Eton in 1954, Lord Robert later at Gordonstoun and the girls at St Mary's, Calne. The tennis court and swimming pool in the walled garden were added attractions for the young people in the holidays and the place began to feel more like home.

From 1956 to 1957, Lord Shelburne was Page of Honour to the Queen. The family already had a page's outfit, so with part of the allowance to obtain one he paid for his pilot's licence training. He spent the remainder on a 1932 Lagonda sold to him for £75 by Eton schoolmaster Willy Gladstone. The Easter holidays then became great fun as this splendid motor car was driven endlessly around on the Bowood roads until it eventually met up with a beech tree. Taking the engine and bent chassis to pieces and putting them together again at the Pinhills workshop (for farm machinery) was almost as much fun as the driving. It was also good to make friends with the sons of Farm Manager Peter Walker who lived at Pinhills.

Lord Shelburne left school early, largely owing to a serious viral illness affecting his liver, not long before Christmas 1958. After a lengthy recovery period, which included a job working in each department at Bowood, it was decided that he should make a complete change and spend some time in Africa.

Arriving in Kenya in March 1959, he stayed at first with his cousin, Pam Scott, soon finding himself a job with David Roberts, an entrepreneur harvesting tilapia fish from Lake Baringo. Each day he would take a boat out and collect the tilapia from the local fishermen on the shores of the lake, bringing them back to the small lakeside factory where they were filleted and frozen. Once a month he drove the frozen packages of fish some 250 miles along a rough dirt track road to Nairobi to be sold. The wild life and birds were fascinating to the young man who had already gained a keen interest in the natural world of Scotland and Wiltshire. David Roberts taught him to hunt crocodiles which led to him being granted a permit to hunt on the Molo River flowing into Lake Baringo. The crocodile skins were sold in Nairobi but they were damaged by button blemishes and there was no fortune to be made from them.

Subsequently, after a period of employment in the Game Department learning the ropes with Head Game Warden Jack Barrah, he was called up into the Kenya Regiment (1960–61). He returned to the United Kingdom aged 21, where he considered what to do next. He had enjoyed two years in Kenya prior to its independence – an amazing experience for a young man sometimes alone with no more than a jeep, a dog and a rifle.

As a boy, Lord Shelburne had given no thought at all to the possibility that Bowood would one day be under his stewardship, but it was now no longer something that he could entirely ignore. It seemed wise to take a deeper interest in the place and in preparation for that he enrolled for a year's course in land management at Cirencester College. After Cirencester, and with an endowment from his American family, he bought some land at Charlcutt, north of Calne, where he began farming cereals on a small scale. He later purchased nearby Catcombe Farm at Spirt Hill, this time with a small dairy herd. Both farms, perhaps 150 acres in total, had once been part of the Bowood Estate.

By 1964, Lord Shelburne had settled down in Wiltshire as a full-time farmer. In that year he became a member of the Calne and Chippenham Rural District Council, which he served until 1973. In October 1965 he married Lady Frances Eliot, sister of his old school friend Lord Peregrine Eliot, and they moved in to newly-purchased and renovated Lower Hangar Farm at Bremhill which, together with Hangar Park Farm bought a year later, made a holding of some 800 acres of land that had also formerly belonged to the Petty-Fitzmaurices. Farm Manager Ian Quant was now employed to help run the farming enterprise which was quite separate from that at Bowood.

Since Lower Hangar Farm House seemed an unimpressive name, Lord Shelburne changed it to Bremhill House, this pomposity causing some confusion for visitors enquiring of local inhabitants the way to the house and being advised, "Never heard of it!"

It was during the Bremhill years that the Shelburnes started their own family: Arabella was born in 1966, then Rachel in 1968, followed by Simon in 1970. Much loved Nanny Cruttenden helped with the children. These were happy times and the young family felt part of the village community. Lord Shelburne was Clerk to Bremhill Parochial Church Council and took on the task of mowing the churchyard. Through local politics and the Church, he got to know many of those living in the Bremhill Division and the parish. Life seemed simple and good fun and their circumstances were particularly fortunate. Though work was hard, there were Mrs Simms to do the cooking and her husband to help in the garden. Later, Bob Darley took over as gardener.

Lord Shelburne maintained an interest in Bowood where he ran the shoot as a syndicate, and a game farm: this, however, was his own operation, run from Bremhill. In this way he got to know the park and woods thoroughly. The rearing pens were set up across Lake Field which probably looked very unsightly below the house although this seemed to be of little concern to his father at the time.

Lord Lansdowne was largely occupied with political life in London, taking time off in Scotland when he could. Although he took an interest in Bowood, he didn't get much involved in a practical way. The Estate Office was still manned by Ted Holman and the estate was left largely to the management of Agent Jack Hickish, who lived at Buckhill House and more or less kept things ticking over. The Estate was making no money: rental incomes were negligible and income had to be raised by selling property. Of 300 cottages owned in 1944, 170 were sold over the following ten years or so.

Lord Lansdowne did, however, take a strong interest in replanting in the park, especially in the rhododendron gardens which he occasionally opened to the public in the 1960s. He first became interested in rhododendrons at Derreen, the estate in Ireland that he had handed over to the Bighams. During the 1960s, with the help of George Harrison and then David Cleverly, he reclaimed the area around the mausoleum and planted some 5 acres of new rhododendrons, many of them having been transplanted from Ford Manor garden in Sussex, following his step-aunt Pauline Spender-Clay's death. The felling and marketing of timber was franchised to Beint & Sons of Studley.

It was while living at Bremhill that Lord Shelburne himself became keenly interested in gardening. This was his second great passion at that time for he had been, for many years, a keen pilot. Having purchased his pilot's licence, he learnt to fly at 16 in a Chipmunk at Scone Airfield, near Meikleour; and when in Wiltshire he flew from Thruxton in a Jackaroo. He was fortunate, with his American endowment, in being able to own an aeroplane of his own. An uncomfortably uneven runway was constructed at Bremhill and the machine was kept in a hangar at the back of the house. When the children were small, the whole family used to fly up to Scotland together for holidays.

In 1969–70, Lord Shelburne took part in the London to Sydney Air Race with co-pilot Flt. Lt. Freddie Laws. The 12,755 mile flight in a Cessna 182E took 94 hours 40 minutes in flying time, grounded for 19 hours owing to mechanical failures and refuelling. On the day before leaving he lunched with his father and mentioned that he'd noticed his obvious affection for Polly Eccles, a close friend. There was no hint of the telegram he was to receive on arrival in Australia on Christmas Eve, saying:

"Congratulations Boy, wonderful achievement! Polly and I were married yesterday."

*Take-off for Australia, 1969: Lady Shelburne standing beside
Lord Shelburne's Cessna 182E*

To spring such a surprise was typical of Lord Lansdowne, who must have guessed that the anxiety of the twelve thousand-odd miles of flying ahead of him would have given his son more pressing things to think about.

In July 1971, Lord Shelburne flew a Beechcraft Bonanza V35A in the London to Victoria, Canada, Air Race, a total of 5,864 miles.

Over time, running the farms on a relatively small scale from Bremhill became a less challenging occupation for Lord Shelburne. He had, however, taken on a number of voluntary roles in local politics as well as serving, since 1963, with the Royal Wiltshire Yoemanry, a Territorial

Army regiment amalgamated with the Royal Yeomanry Regiment in 1971. Having gone into local politics at the age of 23, he had gradually taken a greater interest in and had come to enjoy it, becoming Chairman of the Public Health Committee on the Rural District Council in 1968 and a Wiltshire County Councillor in 1970. In 1972 he was Chairman of the Rural District Council and of the North Wiltshire Steering Committee of Local Government Reorganisation. From 1972 to 1978 he was a member of the South West Economic Planning Council and of the Working Committee on Population and Settlement Patterns. He had also been a Member of the Chippenham Conservative Association since 1964 and thus it came about that he began to consider standing as a Conservative Member for Parliament.

As a first step, the Shelburnes decided to move to Hampshire where it appeared there might be a better opportunity for a Conservative seat. They found a house that they liked and mulled over the particulars before Lord Shelburne informed his father of their plans in May 1971.

Lord Lansdowne was taken unawares. His life was then at a turning point as Lady Lansdowne had expressed her strong dislike of living in more than one place, constantly travelling between London, Bowood and Meikleour. Of his homes, Bowood was his least favourite, possibly because he had never been able to devote enough time to making the Estate a success. He was strongly drawn to and intended to retire to Meikleour, his childhood home. He suddenly realised that if Lord Shelburne were to leave Wiltshire to start a new career and put down roots elsewhere, he would be saddled with the dilemma of what to do with Bowood when he retired – something he was now ready to do. Thus he was precipitated into making Lord Shelburne the offer of Bowood, which, in turn, took the Shelburnes completely by surprise.

Chapter three

Lord Shelburne takes on the Bowood challenge

Although the immediate offer of Bowood was unexpected, Lord Shelburne was eager to make a go of it. Family tradition and obligations were still a matter of course, even in those days. It would be a great privilege, not only to live in beautiful surroundings but also to be the custodian of something that, because of its exceptional qualities, was of intrinsic value to the many people with whom these things might be shared. Making it all work, however, was going to be a challenge. At 31, Lord Shelburne was young and confident, and had some years of experience in farming and administration behind him. He already knew and loved the place. With hindsight, he may have been over enthusiastic, for the task proved in some ways to be a poisoned chalice. For a start, taking over the reins was far more complicated than he had expected.

Lord Lansdowne, eschewing the business side of the hand-over, left everything to his lawyers. All correspondence on the matter between father and son was conducted by letter or through solicitors and accountants. A Court Order was made to break the complex Trust set up by the 5th Marquess, so that parts of the estate could pass to Lord Shelburne while his father was still alive. Some property and chattels thus came directly into Lord Shelburne's ownership while other parts of the estate, including the house and pleasure grounds, remained tied up in Trusts. The 7th Marquess' Will Trust remained active, so that a number of the most important Bowood family possessions still belonged to Lord Lansdowne, including those he had already removed to Meikleour – among them the family jewellery. Thus an enormously cumbersome situation arose from the Trusts which, had he been better informed at the time, Lord Shelburne would have argued strongly against.

The financial situation soon became apparent. The Estate business was making a loss. Lord Lansdowne had been financing his own and necessary Estate expenditure with sales of property, pictures and other valuable possessions. Over time, and partly owing to his commitments elsewhere, he had found it easier to raise capital through sales and shelve underlying longer-term problems.

In 1972, Lord Shelburne took on the running of the Bowood farms. He was obliged to buy out his father's 'farming investments' in the Estate for the sum of one hundred and twenty thousand pounds, which he was able to do with part of his inheritance from his mother. In protesting to his father at this rather excessive demand, he received the reply: "No, no, no Boy, it's just redistribution of wealth within the family!"

The problems ahead were both numerous and considerable. Independent advice from his lawyer, who was sure it wouldn't be possible to keep Bowood together with the conditions Lord Shelburne had to accept, was: "You shouldn't touch it with a barge pole: there isn't a hope of this place ever being able to stand in its own feet." For a start, there was no revenue stream; then there was a huge liability, added to which was the constant handicap of all the legal restraints that would cause endless difficulties over the years to come. Nevertheless, undaunted by these drawbacks, Lord Shelburne pressed ahead and he and Lady Shelburne began to make preparations to move.

One of the first tasks before the move was to assess the condition of the house and undertake necessary repairs, including some re-roofing. Four staff flats were formed in and adjoining the northwest tower of the stable courtyard. Alterations to the house included the creation of a nursery wing and a playroom. The principal rooms on the ground and first floors were redecorated; the kitchen and some of the bathrooms were modernized; and a new oil-fired boiler was installed. These works were undertaken by Hugh Roberts' Bath architectural firm; mostly completed in 1972, they were not quite finished when the family arrived.

The Shelburnes settled in at Bowood in February 1973 with their three young children: Arabella, Rachel and Simon, and Nanny Cruttenden. Their second son, William, was born later that year. There was a skeleton staff to help with running the house, including Mrs Simms, who did the cooking. Bremhill House, the former family home, was initially let; it was sold in 1997 together with some of the adjoining farmland. As a consequence of the re-organisation of the Estate, Lord Shelburne now owned some 760 acres of land in his own right, including the dairy, beef and heifer farms to the north and northwest of Bowood which were amalgamated to become Hangar Park Farms.

Lord Shelburne's own lifestyle had, up to this point, been remarkably free from financial and other worries. The income from his mother's legacy had made it possible to own his own house and run his farming enterprise. His responsibilities at Bowood had now widened considerably and, in view of his enthusiasm for flying, he was particularly anxious to ensure that his family would always be adequately provided for and that the future of Bowood would be as secure as practicable. He straight away made the necessary legal arrangements.

Another key task was to make inventories of the contents of Bowood. The schedule of chattels gifted to Lord Shelburne by his father was brief and there was clearly a great deal else besides – from the attics to the cellars, in storerooms and barns. New schedules were compiled, not only for the purpose of knowing what there was but also for insurance.

To ensure that the principal works of art in the house might be formed into a collection that could be securely kept together, the Bowood Collection Trust was conceived and finally set up in 1974. The new Collection Trust comprised many items not already protected under the pre-existing Will Trust, such as books and other important pictures and furniture. Once again, however, the advice given at the time proved to be unhelpful in later years.

Lord Shelburne was also concerned about the highly important Bowood archives in the muniment rooms. These papers, belonging to the Will Trust, included the political papers of the 1st and 3rd Marquesses and some remaining papers of the 5th Marquess, all three of whom had been leading statesmen. In addition, there were the papers of Sir William Petty, 17th-century inventor and polymath, who had founded the family fortune: these too were of major importance to scholars. Lord Shelburne arranged for all of these documents to be microfilmed by the Bodleian Library over a period of some years from 1975 onwards. The Petty papers were catalogued by Doreen Slatter who held the post of Archivist at Bowood from 1979 to 1984.

The stables at Bowood, c.1977

The library at Bowood, 1998 (Jarrold & Sons Ltd.)

Work began, with only a small workforce, on getting the Estate into better order. Very few of Lord Lansdowne's staff remained; many had retired or took jobs elsewhere, including Resident Agent Jack Hickish who was replaced by John Wallis who ran his own firm and on a part-time basis worked closely with Lord Shelburne. Marcus O'Lone and Clive Knowles-Jackson were among those who worked successively as full-time Assistant Agents under the guidance of John Wallis. Changes were made not only to the staff but also to the running of the Estate and the Estate Office. Over time, as the new regime was established and new enterprises were introduced, more staff began to be employed in different departments.

Ted Holman who had kept the books in the Estate Office was replaced by Mrs Whittle. Sheila McKnight, who had been Lord Shelburne's mother's Private Secretary, worked for him in his office in the house until 1975 when a new office and farm office were created in the present Estate Office yard.

Two men worked full-time and others part-time or self-employed in the Buildings department on general maintenance, initially under Foreman John Gardiner. Skilled tradesmen included carpenter John Harrison and painter and decorator Frank Onslow who repainted the library and chapel ceilings. Jim Stewart, who had worked for the Estate for most of his life, was also one of the team until he retired. A system of five-year programmes of maintenance and repairs was set up. At first, some of this work was undertaken by Rendells of Devizes but to save on costs, the Bowood team was expanded to six men who thereafter took care of all of the estate maintenance. The only government building repair grant Bowood received was for restoration of the domed mausoleum roof. As a condition, this Grade I Listed building standing in the rhododendron gardens had to be opened to the public for six weeks a year.

The mausoleum at Bowood

Head Gardener Derek Duck continued to cultivate the gardens close to the house with assistant Dougie Morse. Bob Darley, who had worked on the garden at Bremhill House, looked after 'Lady Lansdowne's Garden', beside the private house, until just before he died in 1978. Two more gardeners were taken on over the following years, once the park and gardens were opened to the public. In 1974 the terrace gardens were renovated and an annual programme of new planting was instigated here and in the pleasure grounds.

George Harrison remained as Head Forester, managing the mixed-species estate woodlands with four assistants, one of whom was David Cleverly who also worked in the pleasure grounds and was appointed Head Groundsman. Tom Curran took over as Head Forester in 1977, while George Harrison continued to work part-time for a few more years. The Forestry department was almost immediately faced with the problems of Dutch elm disease which continued apace throughout the late 1970s. Apart from clearing and planting new trees, much re-fencing was needed.

In 1973 the timber cutting for saleable wood was still franchised to W.E. Beint & Sons, of Studley. Lord Shelburne set up an estate sawmill at The Osprey in the 1970s and by 1980 the Forestry department was self-supporting. Beints continued to cut large Bowood oak butts for planking for many years; that job is now (2016) undertaken by the Vastern Timber Co. Ltd. The planks are stored at The Osprey until dried out, and then cut in the Bowood mill and used for specific jobs on the estate.

The shoot, already managed by Lord Shelburne in 1973, was let and continued under the care of Head Gamekeeper Mike Paget, who lived at Kennels Lodge. He had a team of three keepers.

Already an experienced farmer, from the early seventies onwards Lord Shelburne began to develop what eventually became a highly successful farming business employing 23 people. In 1972 there were two small dairies, at Pinhills and Home Farm. Under Farm Manager Richard Harward, milk production was expanded to four dairies by the late 1970s when farming was becoming commercially profitable and the estate was beginning to generate enough money to keep the house going. As tenants retired, land was taken back in hand, beef production was expanded and eventually some 2,500 acres were under cultivation, with Home Farm as the centre of operations in the park.

After the UK joined the European Economic Community in 1973, there was a generous system of Government grants, partly subsidised by Europe, for all kinds of agricultural projects, from the removal of hedges to putting up buildings. In 1979 the new, open-plan Tossels Farm Dairy for about 200 cows, built by F. Rendell & Son of Devizes, won the Country Landowners Association Award for the best-designed dairy building.

In order to maintain a close managing interest in the work of the estate, Lord Shelburne early on adopted a management technique which has remained largely unchanged. While he was involved in local government, he had greatly admired Irwin Bellow (subsequently Lord Belwin), Leader of Leeds City Council, whose advice to him was: "Two things I always do: I appoint my own staff and I sign all the bills". That advice was followed.

Fortnightly meetings with heads of departments and monthly financial meetings were introduced. Further regular meetings were needed as the Estate business became more diverse over time; and nowadays it is necessary to delegate a number of day-to-day management and financial tasks to others. Careful minutes are kept but it is always vital to know your staff in person, for you must employ the right people whose skills can be relied upon. An annual meeting of the Bowood Trustees keeps them advised of what goes on and allows them to consider relevant proposals and expenditure.

Going back to 1973, one of the priority tasks was to continue the work of getting the many estate cottages and other buildings back into good order. Lord Lansdowne had made a start on this with capital raised from building the first phase of new housing at Derry Hill in the 1960s which, along with sales of other local property, had also helped to keep the Estate afloat. When Lord Shelburne took over, however, there were still some 50 out of 120 cottages with no proper kitchens, inside lavatories or baths. Further sales were necessary to pay for repairs and refurbishment largely undertaken by Rendells. Some 40 cottages, whose retention was unviable owing to low controlled rents, were sold in outlying villages such as Bremhill and Pewsham. At the same time, it became necessary to consider the potential for housing developments on suitable land, including the possibility of extending the new development begun by Lord Lansdowne at Derry Hill and Studley. Opportunities for such development here and elsewhere were – and indeed continue to be – under continual appraisal.

The national political and economic situation had and still has a direct impact on the financing and management of a large estate like Bowood. Monetary policy under the Heath Government and joining the European Common Market created a boom which stimulated the Organization of the Petroleum Exporting Countries (OPEC) into forming a cartel which successively increased the price of oil, by as much as four times within a year in 1974. A rapid rise in the rate of inflation and in the cost of goods and necessary commodities created problems for everyone and led to a rise in the power of the Trades Unions and the three-day week in 1974. The cost of living at Bowood became almost untenable, especially with controlled rents and little income from the estate in the early years before farming became profitable. If sales of property were to continue in order to keep things afloat, then there would eventually be nothing left. So it became necessary to look at diversification, and by the end of 1973 thoughts turned to the possibility of opening to the public.

Chapter four

Opening to the public: sharing and creating more for visitors to enjoy

The reasons for opening Bowood were twofold: it seemed wrong to live in such an exceptional place and not to share it with others; at the same time, there was a need to cover some of the running costs of the Estate. It was decided to start cautiously at first, so that the enterprise could be gradually expanded as experience was gained. The rhododendron gardens area of the park had been occasionally opened to visitors in earlier years, with proceeds going to local charities, and this practice was continued.

As a member of the Historic Houses Association, Lord Shelburne visited owners of private houses open to the public and gained ideas by talking with them and seeing what they were doing. It soon became obvious that income from opening to visitors would do little more than assist with running costs and never amount to their totality.

The pleasure grounds were first opened for a limited number of days in 1975. A small admissions kiosk was set up at Temple Gate and mobile lavatories were located behind the laurels on the way down to the house. There was a refreshments caravan, from which soft drinks and snacks were sold, and new seats and tables were made by John Harrison in the Estate Carpenter's workshop. Promotion and advertising were organized – including television, posters and flyers. The first catalogue of trees in the arboretum was produced. Most of the tasks were undertaken by existing staff at first but it was necessary to take on dedicated staff in later years.

Overall expenditure for opening in 1975, including capital costs, amounted to nearly four times the income. During that year plans were under way for opening some of the house in the following year. At that time, about half of the house complex was derelict. The orangery and chapel were opened to visitors in 1976 and two years later the library and laboratory were included. A brochure was produced in 1976 giving an account of the house and gardens.

For the second season, the gardeners' bothy, originally built at the beginning of the century as accommodation for young gardeners, was turned into a café with wheel chair access. Work was undertaken on improving the gardens and the pleasure grounds. Species with a long flowering season, such as floribunda roses and geraniums, were planted on the terraces, while numerous trees and shrubs were added to the pleasure grounds and arboretum. Thousands of daffodils and narcissi were planted in Lake Field in the late seventies, between the house and the lake, and garden produce was sold to visitors during the open season. New planting has continued to the present day.

Daffodils in Lake Field (Sir Geoffrey Shakerley, 1979)

A major innovation was the July 1978 installation of David Wynne's large marble statue, *The Reclining Woman*, overlooking the Bowood terraces. She replaced a 19th-century statue of a river god with attendants by C.R. Smith that had become so weathered that it was almost unrecognizable and impossible to restore.

After seeing the adventure playground at Ragley Hall in Warwickshire, Lord Shelburne decided to replicate a similar concept in the pleasure grounds. During the winter months of 1977–78 work began on the Bowood adventure playground – a project that has developed over the years into one of the principal attractions and the main source of income for the Open Days department. The first swings and slides were built by Ian Clark and David Cleverly. Later on, under the skilled leadership of boat builder Alastair Guy, more challenging play equipment was constructed using estate timber, with new features being introduced each year.

The adventure playground (Sir Geoffrey Shakerley, c.1983)

There were 18,000 visitors in 1975. Bowood was open for 106 days in 1976 when visitor numbers increased to 25,000, possibly because people were drawn to see the additional attractions; by 1977, opening four days a week, they had dropped to 15,000, from which low point they began to rise again. In 1978 opening was extended to six days a week during the season and, with the adventure playground newly opened, there were 31,000 visitors.

One April day in 1977 Lord Shelburne was looking out of his office window at a group of visitors trudging towards the house in the rain and a cold wind. There was not going to be much of the house for them to see; they were probably hungry and would need to return to the pleasure grounds for refreshments in the bothy. He felt justifiably uneasy and realized that if opening to the public were ever going to work properly, a good deal more ought to be offered.

This could surely be done by converting the derelict part of the house to provide more to look at and much better facilities – something he had been turning over in his mind for some time. There were a great many fascinating family possessions that visitors would love to see. Some of these treasures, hidden away in the cellars and storerooms of the house, were in poor condition; while a fine collection of Classical and 19th-century sculpture abandoned in the disused stables and a barn also needed conservation.

From then onwards, a major project was in gestation; but the first consideration was to find the money for it. The sale to the nation in 1979 of Esteban Murillo's *Don Justino de Neve* provided the bulk of the required capital raised from a single source. This stunning portrait, once part of the 3rd Marquess' collection, is now owned by the National Gallery.

The Murillo had been included within the Bowood Collection Trust. Thus, not only would Capital Gains Tax have to be paid on the sale but Lord Shelburne would have to pass chattels of his own to the Trustees to the value of the painting, thus incurring more tax. It was ironic that so much tax was paid in order to provide something for the public to enjoy. The terms of the Trust had given rise to problems with finance and flexibility only a few years after it had been set up; and the same problems would occur in future, when capital would be needed for Bowood projects. With hindsight, it would have been wiser to leave some of the less pre-eminent art works unencumbered, outside the Trust and remaining in Lord Shelburne's possession, so that only he would have to pay tax if a sale were necessary.

The planning for and execution of the new venture was to take some years, from 1977 to the opening of the upper exhibition rooms for the 1980 season.

Don Justino de Neve, portrait in oils by
B.E. Murillo, 1665 (Sir Geoffrey Shakerley)

Lord Shelburne worked with Bath architect Hugh Roberts on suggestions for conversion of the ground floor stable wings into a kitchen, restaurant and sculpture gallery. The southwest corner tower of the stable courtyard, formerly staff accommodation and now derelict with stabling on the ground floor, was proposed for conversion into a shop downstairs with two floors of exhibition rooms above and extending partly over the new restaurant.

Planning permission and Listed Building Consent were finalised in December 1978 and a project team was set up under the leadership of architects' firm Hugh Roberts, Graham & Stollar. The team included representatives of the main contractor, T. Holdoway & Sons Ltd., and sub-contractors as appropriate, along with Bowood Curator Hugh Belsey, who liaised with Lord Shelburne on the project as well as undertaking cataloguing and selecting objects for display. Hugh was assisted by Judith Howard, a ceramics specialist, who worked part-time. Project meetings were held fortnightly as work progressed. James Lomax took over as Curator in 1980 and worked primarily on completion of the exhibition rooms. It was originally intended to finalise the whole project for opening during the 1979 season, to coincide with the Country Landowners Association Game Fair at Bowood in July that year, but it was found impossible to meet this deadline and only the ground-floor conversion was ready in time.

In terms of structural alterations, the changes to the single-storey south stable wing were probably the most radical. This area had originally been designed by Adam to house the 1st Marquess' private zoo, facing north into the stable courtyard. With its false windows, it appeared on the south side to be a continuation of the orangery. The aspect of this space was now to be changed entirely: the stable doors on the north side were to be blocked off and windows opened up to the south. A new sculpture gallery was created: a bright and spacious room looking out on to the terraces. Sculptures from the house, stables and an estate barn were repaired and conserved before being placed in their new locations, the larger ones with the help of forklifts. Two very fine Brussels tapestries depicting scenes from the life of Cyrus, formerly hanging at Lockinge House, were bought by Lord Shelburne to hang on the north wall.

The sculpture gallery at Bowood (Christopher Chard)

New openings were made from the sculpture gallery to the new hall and to the shop and restaurant. The new hall, originally an open archway to the stable courtyard, had been blocked off on the south side when the upper terrace was constructed in 1818. The 1979 conversion now made it possible to cross the new hall from the sculpture gallery to the orangery, giving access from the newly-created rooms into the main house. The doors on both sides of the new hall were furnished with Adam-style door panels from the great drawing room of the Big House demolished in 1955. A new door with etched glass panels bearing the Shelburne monogram and Lansdowne arms was made in the north arch of the new hall to create a formal public entrance to the house.

The restaurant, with seating for 120, was formed out of the west stable wing. The wooden stalls were removed, leaving only the central pillars, and a row of new windows was made in the architectural recesses along the west outer wall. The ground floor of the northwest tower, formerly a tack room, provided space for the restaurant kitchen and ancillary storerooms. New furniture was purchased, and pictures were brought from the picture store to hang on the walls.

The shop was created on the ground floor of the southwest tower, which had formerly been part of the stables: new windows were made in the west and south walls, as well as a door to the upper terrace. Lavatories, including one for the disabled, were sited to each side of a corridor from the shop to the restaurant and between the shop and the sculpture gallery where a new staircase to the exhibition rooms was formed.

The exhibition rooms were one of the most important features of the stables conversion, for their purpose was to provide a backdrop to the history of the Lansdownes. Here it was planned to display a selection of heirlooms and precious objects of all kinds in a chronological succession of small rooms and showcases celebrating the fashions, interests and possessions of the family. Most of these works of art would have been enjoyed in the Big House before it was lost: now they would be seen again at Bowood. Items were selected from the storerooms and many were found to need conservation and repairs. The ivory palace and pagodas shown with the Indian exhibits, for example, were in hundreds of pieces and were painstakingly reassembled by Guy Strutt who, in retirement, undertook the task simply for the pleasure of doing it.

The exhibition rooms were planned around the displays that were to go into them, in the style of each period represented, and decorated under the guidance of Fiona Merritt for interior designers Charles Hammond. In some instances, furnishings from the Big House were brought out of store and used to give greater authenticity: for example, the doors and chimneypiece in the Georgian Room.

The first floor is devoted to the Georgian and Victorian periods of the 1st, 3rd and 5th Marquesses. The fine 18th-century costumes and Lord Byron's Albanian costume were retrieved for the Georgian Room and Byron Case from the Bath Museum of Costume, to which they had been lent by Lord Lansdowne. Queen Victoria's wedding chair, given by her to the 3rd Marquess, is one of the principal objects shown in the Victorian Room. The 5th Marquess' time as Viceroy of India (1888–94) is represented in a number of show rooms and wall cases, where fine inlaid furniture, silver and ivory objects, and a host of other fascinating items brought back by him from India and Burma are displayed against richly coloured silk and fine Oriental textiles.

19th-century Burmese Buddha (Jarrold & Sons Ltd.)

On the top floor, in the southwest tower, a central showcase divided into three compartments, was designed to show the magnificent jewellery and orders presented to Admiral Lord Keith, great grandfather of the 5th Marquess; a display of family miniatures; and a cabinet of medals and orders awarded to members of the Lansdowne family. Nowadays, this last cabinet contains the superb Napoleonic Collection presented for display at Bowood by the 8th Marquis in 1995.

The exhibition rooms and corridors were purposely decorated and furnished to give the feel of a country house interior, so that the displays would be seen as far as possible as they might have been in the Big House. The walls are hung throughout with an outstanding collection of watercolours, chosen to complement the displays, most of them purchased by Lord Shelburne in the 1970s and early 1980s specifically for that purpose. Twentieth-century watercolours of Bowood on the lower staircase walls are followed by 19th-century watercolours of India and Burma to provide an introduction to the 5th Marquess' Indian showcases. A Burmese marble Buddha was placed on the mezzanine landing beside a doorway to a small balcony overlooking the sculpture gallery. The balcony was originally intended to lead to a corridor on the north wall of the gallery where watercolours would be displayed. In the event, that plan was abandoned, for bright light through the south-facing windows might have damaged the fragile paintings.

Malmesbury Abbey,
watercolour by
J.M.W. Turner, 1794
(Jarrold & Sons Ltd.)

On the first floor walls are portrait engravings and miniatures of family members, and watercolours of India and Burma, including some that belonged to the 5th Marquess. At the end of the first floor corridor, British watercolours by 19th-century painters that had belonged to the 3rd Marquess are shown alongside others bought by Lord Shelburne. A similar grouping of mainly 19th-century watercolours is hung on the staircase to the top exhibition room where there is a magnificent display of drawings and watercolours by Richard Parkes Bonington purchased by the 3rd Marquess. Art historian James Miller was commissioned to produce a *Catalogue to the Paintings at Bowood*, published in 1982.

The restaurant, shop and sculpture gallery were opened for the 1979 season, so that they might be used during the July Game Fair which will be considered in the next chapter. The Prince of Wales had agreed to open the stables conversion on his visit to the Game Fair but the conversion was incomplete and the plaque that had been engraved for the occasion bore the wrong date. He quipped that the word "not" should be inserted before "opened by the Prince of Wales"! The plaque is still at Bowood: reversed and bearing a memorial to gardener Bob Darley, it is now on the wall of Lady Lansdowne's Garden where he worked during his last years.

Chapter five

The 1979 Game Fair, politics, and business expansion

A successful Country Landowners Association Game Fair had previously been held at Bowood in 1967. Preparations for the Game Fair on 26–28 July 1979 had begun two years earlier when Lord Shelburne was asked by the CLA if he would host their first three-day event – which would give good publicity to Bowood, as well as fulfilling the intended purpose of helping to extend awareness of country recreational pursuits enjoyed by a diverse group of country lovers.

The running of Bowood was put almost on hold during the weeks before and after this major event. The stalls, pens, and exhibition and action-display areas were laid out in front of the house and down towards the lake. Cars were parked on the large field southwest of the house. The weather, being extraordinarily hot and dry, allowed three full days of enjoyment and, incidentally, saved the grass from being churned up by vehicles.

The Fair was opened by the Prince of Wales, who planted a commemorative *Cedrus atlantica* beside the walled garden and overlooking the lake. The three days were considered to have been an enormous success, welcoming a record 113,000 visitors. The CLA paid for some road repairs for improved access, as well as some new fencing, but no share of the profits came to Bowood. A week after the event, it poured with rain and the grass was transformed: one would hardly have known so many people had walked and driven across it.

1979 was an extremely busy year for Lord Shelburne. Apart from planning for the Game Fair and overseeing the stables conversion scheme, he stood as Conservative candidate for Coventry North East in the general election. He had spent two days a week for the past two years canvassing some 43,000 people in Coventry, with a marvellous team of supporters, including Constituency Chairman Alan Tandy and his wife Jean.

Since taking on Bowood, Lord Shelburne had maintained his interests in local and national politics and he had previously been shortlisted as a parliamentary candidate for Winchester and for Epsom and Ewell. In addition to his role on the Parish Council, he became a member and then chairman of the South West Economic Planning Council and its Working Committee on Population and Settlement Patterns. His particular skills and interests in housing and tenancies were developed from his Rural District Council days in the mid seventies, at a time when home ownership was less than 40 per cent. He had helped to create a housing scheme sidestepping the Labour Government's restrictions on tenancies and enabling short-term lettings to be made. From around 1977 he worked for two years as an advisor on local government affairs and was involved in the concept of the 'right to buy' which ultimately gave rise to incorporation of the right to buy in the Housing Act 1980. Some 60 to 70 per cent of tenants, including those in poorly-maintained council-monopoly estates, were then given the chance to buy their own homes. It was these and other long-standing political interests that had led Lord Shelburne's continuing interest in standing for Parliament but it was, perhaps, just as well for Bowood that he was unsuccessful.

A less happy outcome of the pressures of the Shelburnes' extremely busy lives was their decision to separate. Lady Shelburne moved to Gloucestershire in 1980 and newly-appointed Housekeeper Hazel Bicknell came to live in Rose Cottage, close to the Estate Office, and took over the running of the private house alongside Mrs Simms who remained as Cook. Nanny Cruttenden who still lived at Bowood, kept an eye on the younger children during the holidays. The children were growing up and could keep in close touch with their mother only a few miles away. The girls were weekly boarders at St Mary's, Calne, while the boys were boarding at prep schools.

In 1978, in preparation for expanded Open Days facilities, the old porter's lodge, just inside the gateway to the house complex, was converted into an office for a House Manager who, from then on, would be responsible for the arrangements for opening to the public. The first to take up the post, in 1979, was Commander Taylor. In that year the new attractions offered on the ground floor of the old stables, including the restaurant, brought a total of 46,000 visitors to Bowood House and Gardens, of which around 10,000 were among the 113,000 attending the Game Fair. Mr Hazell, a local man, was Bowood's 100,000th visitor in July.

Bowood restaurant opened 1979 (Sir Geoffrey Shakerley, 1979)

Access for the larger numbers of visitors coming to Bowood each year required careful management of increased full and part-time staff employed in opening to the public, along with ensuring that publicity, presentation, health and safety, catering and supplies, and many other relevant aspects were adequately provided for. Open Days meetings were now held fortnightly with heads of departments, in addition to the fortnightly 'Timesheet' meetings, in order to plan operational activities and work to be undertaken. By 1989 there were around 50 full- and part-time seasonal staff employed in the Open Days business enterprise. Monthly Estate meetings with heads of departments continued, to ensure the financial side of the business was managed effectively, with regular presentation of the figures by the Financial Controller who assembled the annual budget at the beginning of each year.

1980 saw the delayed opening of the new suite of exhibition rooms in May, and the publication of a new Bowood guidebook with photographs by Sir Geoffrey Shakerley. Now all of the stables conversion project could be enjoyed by visitors who numbered 42,770 that year. The licensed restaurant was made available for conferences and other functions; while among the wide range of items on sale in the gift shop were Bowood souvenirs, such as china plates, mats and trays, and prints of watercolours of Bowood by local artist G.A. Renvoize.

Souvenir plate with transfer printed drawing of Bowood by Graham Rust, 1977

Sally Crossland took over from Commander Taylor as House Manager in July 1980 and remained in post for another seven years, assisted by Jane Meadows (née Ward) from 1984. Jane remained as Assistant House

Manager under Anna Blundell who left in 1990 but was to return to the job some years later. Jane, now one of the longest-serving of Bowood's staff, continues to help out occasionally to the present day, despite having taken early retirement in 2009.

Following the opening of the exhibition rooms, the cost of opening Bowood to the public in 1980–81 came to just over double the revenue generated. By the end of the 1982 season, after opening hours had been extended to all day, visitor numbers had increased to around 100,000: nearly 50 per cent more than in 1981 and bucking the trend in private houses open to the public elsewhere in the country. Liz Fox took over as Catering Manageress in the Restaurant in 1982 and started to make this enterprise profitable. Her Bowood shortbread, Carlsbad plums and game pies were early favourites and also sold well in the gift shop. Liz retired in 1990 and was succeeded by Lynne Rawlings whose home baking was equally popular.

Admiral Lord Keith at the Battle of Muizenberg (1795), portrait in oils by H.P. Danloux, 1801

The first of the Bowood special exhibitions was mounted in the orangery for the 1982 season by new part-time Curator Fiona Pilkington, with assistance from James Lomax. The display of family portraits, archives and memorabilia about Admiral Lord Keith (1746–1823), was the first of such exhibitions on subjects relating to Bowood and the Lansdownes which would provide something new and informative for visitors to see each year, including many items from the private house that would otherwise not be on public display. During the 1980s, themes included Dr Johnson and the Thrales (Hester Thrale was Lord Keith's second wife) and, from 1987, under the curatorship of Kate Fielden, Sir William Petty, 17th-century scientist, inventor, founder of the family fortune and the first to map Ireland efficiently; the history of the garden at Bowood; and the 5th Marquess as Viceroy of India.

Sir William Petty, portrait in oils by J.Closterman, c.1680 (Jarrold & Sons Ltd)

The renovation of the bothy 'Garden Tea Room' in 1982–83, and again in 1986, provided further accommodation and generated a welcome increase in turn-over. In 1985, the old apple store against the walled garden close to the bothy and adventure playground was converted into conveniently located lavatories with the help of a Countryside Commission grant. The total number of visitors to Bowood in 1983 was 79,716: fewer than in 1982 but once more exceeding the national trend in private country-house visiting. Numbers increased to nearly 114,000 in 1984 with the fine weather continuing into 1987 when there were some 176,500 visitors, the largest number in any year before or since. By this time, income from the Open Days enterprise was going a long way towards defraying the costs of maintaining the house, gardens and pleasure grounds. In the late 1980s, visitor numbers began to fall but remained at over 150,000 per annum until 1990, when they decreased to 121,569. The downward trend reflected an increase in competing local attractions as well as the effects of high interest rates and the advent of cheaper package holidays. The last factor, in particular, had given rise to social changes as families were able to take holidays abroad, often for the first time. The weather, of course, continued to be a major influencing factor.

The gardeners' bothy, converted to a cafe (1977) and party rooms (2002)

The adventure playground was considerably enlarged during the 1980s. Repair and construction work was undertaken in the winter months by Alastair Guy, who lived in a caravan on-site, with some assistance from Bowood craftsmen. The *Centaur* ship was built in the winter of 1982–83 and the helter-skelter and 'death slide' in 1984–85. An all-weather grass surface was laid for the 1986 season; and a flume (metal tube) slide was constructed in 1987 which proved so popular that two more were added in 1988. During the 1988–89 closed season, safety nets were placed under the walk-ways between climbing features and slides. In 1989 a new area was created with play equipment dedicated to younger children and toddlers; more was added to this play area in 1990 and in the same year a 'flying fox' was set up for use by older children under supervision. This annual succession of new features for children was a considerable attraction and brought many more young visitors. Families could spend the whole day here during the school holidays, bringing picnics to eat on the grass or buying refreshments from the nearby Garden Tea Room. Parents are expected to look after their own children's safety in the playground but since the 1980s Bowood has employed a team of young people during the holidays, usually local school leavers, to ensure that the equipment is being used properly and to assist if necessary.

With the expansion of the Open Days operation, it was decided that a more appropriate reception area should be built at the visitors' entrance beside the car park. Proposals were considered for a garden centre building which would incorporate a ticket desk and lavatories, sell local gift products and provide some introductory information about Bowood. Architectural firm Graham Moss Associates designed a 30m-square natural timber-framed and glass-sided pavilion, for which planning permission was given in January 1983. Grants from the English Tourist Board and the Countryside Commission made it possible to proceed and the facility was partially opened in 1983 and fully operational for the 1984 season. The Bowood Forestry department provided some of the timber used for the building. A formal guide to *Bowood's Trees and Shrubs*, by botanist Allen J. Coombes, was published to coincide with the

Garden Centre opening in 1983.

Soft fruit and vegetables from the farm had been on sale to the public since 1982 but a new Pick-Your-Own enterprise was set up in 1983: alongside the car park, it became an appropriate adjunct to the Garden Centre Shop managed by Maureen Taylor which, before the Sunday Trading Act in 1994, was able to sell garden produce and plants on Sundays. The gift shop in the house (renamed the Terrace Shop) did less well in competition with the newly-opened Garden Centre. By 1986, the Garden Centre was kept open during the winter months when the house and gardens were closed.

The Garden Centre, c.1984

In 1988, after Maureen Taylor had moved to the south of the county, plantsman Peter Edmonds took over in the Garden Centre. Following Lord Shelburne's marriage to his second wife in 1987, the Garden Centre and Terrace Shops were run by Lady Shelburne and her Personal Assistant Nicky Thomas. Lady Shelburne's professional skills as an interior designer led to a marked change in the focus of goods on sale which was highly successful. In addition to managing the Bowood shops, she ran her own interior design business, Fiona Shelburne, working for private clients all over the country and abroad: an enterprise which continues to this day. Her touch is seen in almost all of the public rooms at Bowood, and she has also been responsible for redecoration of many of the private rooms in the house.

During his State Visit from 23 to 26 October 1984, it was arranged for President and Mme Mitterrand to spend a day at Bowood, where they could relax and enjoy the surroundings of an English country house and garden. That they should visit Bowood was especially appropriate owing to the strong historic connections of the Lansdowne family with France, culminating in the signing of the *Entente Cordiale* by the 5th Marquess and President Loubet in 1902. In more recent times, the 8th Marquis had served as a liaison officer under General Leclerc during the War and as Secretary to the British Ambassador in France immediately afterwards. The Mitterrands' helicopter arrival was greeted on the terraces by Lord Shelburne and his family, and a welcoming group of some 600 local people, including children from Derry Hill School. Following a private lunch in the house, Lord Lansdowne gave a speech in French and Lord Shelburne was presented with the order of *Officier de la Légion d'honneur* by President Mitterrand. In the afternoon, the Mitterrands planted a hornbeam, *Carpinus betulus* 'Pyramidalis' close to the cedar planted by the Prince of Wales in 1979.

Shortly before the visit of President and Mme Mitterrand to Bowood, Wendy Leavey took over as Lord Shelburne's Private Secretary and was immediately immersed in the arrangements for the Mitterrands' visit. Having been involved in parish affairs, she was familiar with a number of Lord Shelburne's local interests. One of her notable achievements was to set up a comprehensive filing system for the increasing volume of paperwork generated by Lord Shelburne's office. She was succeeded by Julia Webb in 1988 who admirably embraced the move to office computerization along with the enormous increase in Lord Shelburne's (Lord Lansdowne from 1999) estate and public activities over the years up to the present day. She has earned the friendly respect of all who come into contact with her.

Computerisation was introduced during the 1980s and the Estate accounting system was streamlined on microcomputer by Financial Controller Tony Bishop in 1985. Sue Hatchard took over from Tony in 1987 and oversaw the installation of an upgraded Accounts computer in 1989. Ted Holman, who had worked in the Estate Office for the 8th Lord Lansdowne, returned in 1985 to catalogue and archive 20th-century estate papers no longer in current use, including some from Lord Shelburne's time.

As the Bowood enterprises began to expand, the workload of Sallyanne Sime who had been employed since May 1980, principally as Personal Assistant to Assistant Estate Managers Jeremy Hulme (1979-84) and Guy Sherratt (1984–85), increased considerably. The new post of Receptionist was introduced, to which Margaret Pollitt was appointed in 1985. Shirley Bennett took over when Margaret moved to work at the Garden Centre Shop in 1989 until 1993. In 1985 Philip Cubbon, who had farmed locally for many years, became Bowood's new Estate Manager. John Wallis continued on a part-time basis as Bowood Agent. When Sallyanne moved to Yorkshire in 1986, her post was filled for shorter periods by a succession of efficient Personal Assistants whose tasks from the late 1980s onwards included looking after the increasing number of Estate lettings: from fishing permits to cottage and farm property rentals.

The annual programme of modernising and repairs to farm and estate buildings continued under a maintenance staff based at The Osprey yard which, by 1988, had increased to nine under Foreman Graham Iles. Some grants were available for repairs, especially for re-roofing. When the Estate farming operations began to be run down in the late 1980s, cottages in Derry Hill, Studley and Sandy Lane slowly became vacant as their occupants sought farming jobs elsewhere or when elderly retired workers on fixed tenancies died. Properties such as these were now far less frequently sold off but instead were renovated for newly retired estate staff or for letting to bring in an alternative source of Estate income.

By 1989, after Graham Iles had left, the maintenance labour force came under the overall supervision of local builder Brian Vines who ran

The Osprey yard, 2016

his own building company. The relationship between B.A.Vines Ltd. and the Estate proved mutually beneficial over following years. It allowed larger building tasks to be undertaken efficiently, such as the conversion of Laggus Farm House from two houses into one, and major repairs to Pinhills Farm House; and for a few isolated cottages to be built on Bowood plots on a shared contract basis.

As early as March 1981, a new phase of building at Redhill, part of Derry Hill village, was under discussion, to include a housing scheme for local people and estate staff, and a village green. These deliberations, with revised plans to meet the particular concerns of villagers, continued for some years until an acceptable scheme was brought forward. Finally, in 1988 land was sold to Persimmon for two successive phases of house building at Redhill, and further land was sold for houses at Wenhill, on the southern outskirts of Calne. These sales were crucial to financing a major new enterprise now being planned for Bowood Park. Also in 1988, the redundant Forest Gate Farm buildings, conveniently situated beside the A4 at Pewsham, were let on a seven-year term, with plans in mind for their eventual conversion to small industrial units.

The Forestry department continued to work partly in tandem with the

Shoot. Clearing and fencing were major tasks in the early years, owing to the rabbit problem. Thinning and planting were carried out on an annual basis. Fence posts and stakes cut for sale were in high demand and provided a steady income to offset other costs. Tom Curran left in 1985 and Peter Rigby, who had previously worked on the farm, replaced him as Head Forester. A band saw was purchased in 1986 which allowed accurate cutting of sawn timber for estate repairs and some timber stock for a wider market. In the later 1980s Christmas tree sales were going well, as was the sale of cut firewood and holly. Mechanisation had, by 1989, considerably increased productivity.

The Shoot continued to do well in the early 1980s, with the sale of oven-ready pheasants to local outlets and in the Bowood shops. In 1987 John Maynard was taken on as a beat keeper. Mike Paget, who moved in 1988 to become Head Keeper at Wilton, was replaced by Roy Dollery whose former job as Under Keeper was left unfilled. In 1989 it was decided to let the shoot for five years which would allow a reduction in day-to-day management, with the two shoot employees retained on a contracted-out basis. This did not prove a successful venture and the 5-year agreement was ended in 1990, at which point John Maynard became part-time Keeper and Warden, and the shoot was let on less restrictive terms.

Probably the most significant change to take place at Bowood in the 1980s was the agricultural decline, principally as a result of Common Agricultural Policy reforms introduced in 1984. This change in farming economy and Lord Shelburne's plans for dealing with it are considered in the next chapter.

Chapter six

Agricultural changes in the 1980s lead to a new enterprise

The Bowood farms were doing well in the early 1980s, enjoying profits in the three years from 1979 to 1981 and a record harvest in 1980. About 2,500 acres were in cultivation or used for grazing for the two dairy herds at Pinhills and Home Farm. Two further dairies were located at Hangar Park, to the north of Bowood, and Tossels, on the southern edge of the estate. In November 1982, when Farm Manager Richard Harward retired and Christopher Duncan took over, there were some 530 milking cows under the care of Foreman Keith Matthews; with 1,530 cattle in total, including rearing and fat stock. The farm continued to perform well in 1983 when larger bulk tanks were installed for milk and the Pinhills dairy was modernised. Although cereal yields were down, potatoes and soft fruit increased in turnover, helped in part by the installation of an irrigation scheme using water from the lake.

In 1984 there was another good harvest with around 1,380 acres of arable selling crops, including 815 acres of wheat, and some 335 acres of forage crops for the cattle. It was planned to increase the soft fruit acreage to about 12 acres in 1985. In the following two years, the dairies continued to do well but cereal harvests were less than satisfactory. This was partly owing to poor weather which affects drainage of the light, greensand soils at Bowood, making them on the whole better for grazing or market gardening rather than arable cultivation. But it also reflected the result of a change in emphasis in land use at Bowood.

Farming in the European Community under the Common

Agricultural Policy (CAP) had, by the late 1970s and early '80s, led to increased prosperity and greater productivity as a result of grant aid and support for all kinds of agricultural activity and its improvement, along with secure markets and prices. This basic system led to over-production and the infamous 'butter mountains' and other surpluses for which no immediate market could be found within Europe. Farmers were still being paid for goods that were simply destroyed on site where markets could not be found or stored for sale on the global market at reduced prices. The CAP reforms brought in from 1984 were an attempt to halt this intolerable situation with, for example, milk quotas and set aside payments being introduced to limit production.

At the same time, by the mid 1980s, improved deep freezing technology as well as the speed and reduction in cost of carriage by air freight allowed reciprocal market trading of agricultural products all over the world, with supermarkets buying in bulk and a corresponding decline in small farms unable to compete in the home market.

The warning bell for the Bowood farming enterprise was sounded with the introduction of CAP reforms. The Estate's farming turnover in 1986 was nearly £2 million, only making a profit of some £7,300. This challenging and highly capitalised business wasn't making much return: the park was being degraded; and tying up so much capital didn't make sense.

Lord Shelburne and his advisers took stock of the situation. The seemingly relentless encouragement of agriculture had led to ever more land in the park being placed under pressure of exploitation, with concomitant impacts on tranquillity and sustainability, not to mention administration costs. Moreover, the Bowood farms were awkwardly dispersed – a disadvantage that became more problematic as farming became less profitable.

It was therefore decided to withdraw substantially from farming and to follow an ambitious new plan involving construction of a golf course on Home Farm land.

Golf was being promoted heavily at this time by the golf industry. The game had become something of a craze: it had always had devotees but more golfers were joining clubs and the game was on the ascendancy, with perhaps two and a half million people now playing in the United Kingdom. There was pent up demand: every club had a long waiting list and a number of new courses were being built. If planning permission could be gained, Bowood clearly had more to offer than other golf courses in the region and perhaps anywhere else.

Owned by a Bowood Trust and rented to Lord Shelburne as a life tenant, like much of the Estate land and many of its cottages, the c.200 acres of Grade 3 agricultural land comprising Home Farm was part of 'Capability' Brown's 18th-century designed landscape, now designated as Grade I parkland. It differed from the main park in always having been divided by hedges for enclosing stock. Nevertheless, it included some fine trees and plantations and there was no doubt about the unique quality of the area and its setting, or its magnificent views to the distant Marlborough Downs.

Apart from the run-down and ugly late 20th-century structures in the farm buildings complex, an attractive Listed farmhouse and barns might be retained and converted into a clubhouse and ancillary facilities; and there was space alongside for further development of an hotel and conference centre at some future time. Access to the golf course and buildings complex could be via Sir Charles Barry's 1845 Golden Gates entrance to the park in Derry Hill, a route now rarely used by the family and not at all by visitors to Bowood House and Gardens. An existing estate road to the farmhouse would give convenient access for service vehicles from the A342.

The vision to realize this entirely separate project in a series of development stages was Lord Shelburne's. It was clear to him that the future of Bowood lay in its enjoyment by visitors and that their increased footfall and spending were vital to success. Diversity would be essential: a variety of attractions would encourage visitors to come from a range of markets: tourism and leisure activities, corporate and business use, private party and wedding functions. The hotel would make it feasible to hold two- or three-day conferences, and to offer opportunities for people to relax for a few days and enjoy the different amenities Bowood has to offer, including a visit to the House and Gardens.

Home Farm, aerial view before re-development (© Skyscan.co.uk, 1989)

From 1987 onwards, in preparation for the new enterprise, the arable farmland of some 1,300 acres producing crops for sale was divided up into blocks and let to around eight local farmers who could thereby spread their overheads and benefit from some extra land. The Estate would now receive secure rents for that land and would no longer have the liabilities or problems inherent in what was becoming a highly uncertain arm of the business. The soft fruit and pick-your-own enterprises were continued for the time being.

The Golden Gates entrance to Bowood Hotel, Spa & Golf Resort, 2016

In 1987, the cereal and potato harvests were again poor and it was decided that beef farming would also be abandoned. Richard Keevil, a local farmer, took over that year from Chris Duncan as part-time Consultant Farm Manager to oversee the four dairies, while the sheep flock was increased to 1,000. The outdated Home Farm dairy was closed down in February 1988, by which time plans to proceed with the expensive golf course project were already under way. There was no doubt that the proposals would result in an enormous visual improvement on the existing derelict farm yard and buildings.

By 1988, cereal farming had ceased and the remaining 1,500 acres of land was down to permanent pasture supporting three dairies and the flock of 1,000 sheep. There were now only four men employed on the farm instead of 23 in 1986. As the farm was run down, redundant farm buildings and cottages no longer required for farm employees could be let. The main income for the Estate was now from the Open Days and Garden Centre operations as well as residential lettings.

An application for change of use of the Home Farm land was granted in December 1988. In May 1989, the final sale of farm equipment took place. The three dairies, still profitable, were now run as separate units. Serviceable modern Home Farm buildings were re-sited to The Waste, close to the village of Sandy Lane, where they could be used for storage and the base for the sheep operation. Unusable buildings, including a modern bungalow, were to be demolished. Pinhills and Laggus Farm Houses were now vacant and ready for major refurbishment prior to letting.

In 1989, the main development activity was centred on the golf course project. Lord Shelburne took the lead throughout, employing George McDonic for specialist advice on planning matters, and Ferguson Mann Architects Ltd, a Bristol conservation architectural firm, for work on building projects, including conversions and refurbishment of the Listed buildings. Advice was also obtained from conservation and landscape architectural firm Derek Latham & Company Ltd. Renowned golf course architect Dave Thomas was appointed in December 1989 to design the 18-hole Bowood course and a practice course to the west of the clubhouse. A detailed case was made, by landscape architectural firm Nicholas Pearson Associates Ltd., for conversion of the Home Farm area of the park to a golf course. English Heritage's scrutiny and agreement of the proposals may have been less strict than it would be nowadays, but its sanction of the scheme was a critical achievement.

Outline planning permission was granted in December 1989 for the golf course, clubhouse and ancillary buildings, and for a 120-bed hotel forming an extension of the same complex. The project was to go forward in stages, with construction of the golf course starting in July 1990, following detailed planning consent in May for the golf course, the clubhouse and the golf practice area.

Finance for the project was also obtained in stages. Initially, capital was raised by building and selling houses, including Bremhill House. Over following years, it was necessary also to sell some important possessions, among them significant documents from the Bowood archive, the life interest in which had been surrendered by his father to Lord Shelburne in 1987, under the terms of the Bowood Will Trust. Once again, these sales of possessions involved huge expense: Capital Gains Tax had to be paid twice: by the Trustees and then by Lord Shelburne in passing to the Trust chattels of similar value in compensation.

Added to the distress of having to part with possessions for the ultimate purpose of keeping Bowood afloat, was the burglary in April 1988 of three pieces from the collection of Admiral Lord Keith's Jewels. These treasures had been presented to the Admiral by the Sultan of Turkey in 1801 for his victory against the French at the Battle of Aboukir, Egypt. The burglary was widely publicised and featured in a BBC TV *Crimewatch* re-enactment. Only one piece was eventually recovered. Insurance funding allowed replicas to be made of the Order of the Crescent and the Chelengk (a plume of diamonds), but the loss of the originals for their historical value and importance to Bowood is incalculable.

On the eve of commencement of the golf course venture, Bowood suffered a devastating blow – one that was experienced right across the county. At around midday on 25 January 1990, the eye of an exceptionally violent storm tore southwest to northeast across the park, with winds of up to 110 mph. Such was its strength that around 600 mature trees were destroyed and many others were damaged and disfigured. One hundred and forty mature trees were lost in the pleasure grounds alone, including nearly all of the cedars and most of the trees that had hitherto survived from 'Capability' Brown's planting in the 1760s, many of them recorded in the *Bowood Tree Guide*. The tallest *Cedrus atlantica* in England, at c.140 feet, was shattered in an instant. In the park, around 500 trees were lost or damaged, notably in the rhododendron gardens; while in the commercial woodlands thousands of semi-mature trees were lost.

This was not the only damage caused by the storm: George Kennedy's 1845 gazebo on the lower terrace was smashed apart by falling pines which also took away some of the balustrade below it. A huge beech tree

73

Great Storm, January 1990: Head Gardener Derek Duck (R) and Head
Groundsman David Cleverly (L) stand beside the fallen Cedrus atlantica
(Richard Pearce)

fell across the opening of the Hermit's Cave beside the lake, destroying a substantial part of its roof. There was considerable structural damage, especially to roofs of estate buildings. Bowood House itself suffered losses of tiles and leadwork, while the game larder in the Estate Office yard, in use as a store, was demolished by a falling tree which also caused serious damage to a number of staff cars. Office and house staff at Bowood took shelter in the house while the storm raged. Roof slates were bowled like playing cards down towards the lake and large pieces of lead crashed to the ground. The reverberations of falling trees were like the sounds of a battle field. Electric power was lost – as were telephone connections. All estate roads were blocked by horrific tangles of fallen trees. By late afternoon, as darkness was falling, office staff were towed in their cars by tractor across the Home Farm fields and out via Studley Gate; while the forestry team had already begun work on clearing the estate roads.

Great Storm 1990: Terrace gazebo destroyed by a Corsican pine
(Richard Pearce)

As buildings were made safe over the following days, it was necessary to take stock. Local photographer Richard Pearce was immediately commissioned to make a record of the storm damage while Bristol & West Photography Ltd. was asked to photograph the estate from the air. An insurance claim of nearly £120,000 was drawn up for repairs to the house and farm buildings alone. The only grant-aid was sought from and given by English Heritage for clearance of storm damaged trees and some re-planting in the park and pleasure grounds.

Barry Lawrence had recently taken over from Peter Rigby as Head Forester. With two full-time forestry assistants and one part-time helper, there were not enough men to deal with the clearing of damaged and fallen trees and a Scottish forestry team was brought in for support. The sellable timber was marketed by Wessex Woodland Management Ltd. but much was lost at a time when there was, inevitably, a timber glut.

Work on the rhododendron gardens was a priority, for it was hoped that they might be opened for the 1990 flowering season. In the event, free entry was allowed to this attraction, as the work on clearing and re-planting had not yet finished. Some experimental work was undertaken in raising fallen trees, a successful example of which can be seen in the adventure playground.

During the year, the game larder was repaired and converted into a new estate Accounts Office. The tumbled stonework of the uninsured gazebo on the lower terrace was raised, numbered and stored in an estate barn and the foundations made safe. The lower terrace balustrade was reinstated and I & J Bannerman were employed to repair the Hermit's Cave.

Serendipitously, Corsican pine seed from trees that fell across the lower terrace had previously been collected and germinated by Farm Secretary Gwyn Comley who presented seedlings as replacements here and in the pleasure grounds. A section of the trunk of the fallen *Cedrus atlantica*, showing its annular rings, was saved for display in the 'Schoolroom' in the old walled garden apple store.

All efforts over the next three months were inspired by the determination to open as usual.

By the spring of 1990 Bowood was ready to welcome visitors. An orangery exhibition of photographs of the storm damage showed, by comparison, how much progress had been made outside with clearing and replanting. Indeed, it was surprising to see how rapidly the park and gardens recovered from their battering, although damage to a number of important trees is noticeable here and there to the present day. The oval of sweet chestnuts at the far end of the visitors' car park, for instance, includes younger trees filling the gaps left by destruction of most of its 200-year-old giants. The disaster would lead to other changes, such as new planting in the rhododendron gardens, giving rise to rewarding renewal and innovation.

Chapter seven

After the storm: building the Golf & Country Club and Kerry Suite in the 1990s

During 1990, while foresters, groundsmen and gardeners laboured to restore the park and gardens, and innumerable building repairs were undertaken, work began in earnest on preparing the ground for the golf course for which outline planning permission had been given in 1989. Detailed consent for construction of the clubhouse was obtained in May 1990 and in November that year it was decided to proceed with Phase I only of the overall project. This involved completion of the course and conversion of Home Farm House to the clubhouse with a link to the Listed barn just east of it to provide ancillary facilities for players and administration over a ground floor total of around 10,000 sq. ft. The Golden Gates entrance to the new Golf & Country Club would require major restoration at the same time.

The course was to be constructed over some 193 acres of parkland formerly in agricultural use and surrounding Queenwood, a picturesque house then let to tenants. The land is bisected by a valley with a stream flowing from west to east, a tributary of which runs from Deer Mead Pond to the east of Brick Kiln Wood, site of the former Bowood Brickworks. The Grade 3 agricultural land of sand over clay had always proved awkward to drain.

Course architect Dave Thomas based his design around the existing mature trees and plantations, all of which were retained, including a fine oak left standing on the 6th fairway. The fairways were planned as separate avenues and, as the course flows through each one, none is visible from another. Low mounds were created for bunkers and raised tees and greens to achieve good visibility to landing areas and greens. The layout includes two loops of nine holes each, starting and finishing at the clubhouse. To the west of the clubhouse there is a driving range and a short par 3 course for warming up, teaching and practice. A putting area was designed in front of the clubhouse where there had formerly been a muddy pond. By careful planting and retention of existing features, the course fits comfortably within the parkland landscape and cannot be overlooked or seen from Bowood House and Gardens.

Bowood Golf Course: constructing the lake on the 4th Hole, 1990

Earth moving began in July 1990 under the supervision of Site Manager Mike Bottomley. Prior to commencement of the main earthworks, public footpaths were re-aligned, overhead cables were put underground and existing mature trees carefully guarded against damage. Reconfiguration of the landscape included removal of one lake and the creation of three small ones. Following completion of the earth moving, bunkers and fully irrigated fairways were constructed. Seeds and young trees were planted in the spring of 1991, including wildflower mixes in selected areas. There would be a year's wait while the ground settled before the course could be used.

Construction work on the clubhouse was under way during 1991. The farmhouse was adapted to include a small kitchen and dining room, with a spike bar and club room on the ground floor. Administrative offices and a board room were formed upstairs, while the attic floor above was converted into a two-bedroom flat for a caretaker. A single-storey link building with a glazed passage between the clubhouse and the east barn provided the golfers' entrance and access to the changing rooms. The barn, open to its timbered roof, became the pro-shop with an adjacent bag and shop store and a shoe cleaning and repairs room. Above a small practice area at the north end of the building is an office for the golf professional. The scheme, by Ferguson Mann Architects, allows the mainly 19th-century Listed buildings in the 'Old English' style favoured by the 3rd Marquess for his farm and estate cottages, to retain their form and overall character. Lady Shelburne's interior design work gives an elegant but comfortable character to the new complex.

Bowood Golf Clubhouse (centre) and Kerry Suite (R), 2003

The completed golf course and clubhouse were officially opened on 23 May 1992 as the Bowood Golf & Country Club, and rapidly gained a good reputation under Lord Shelburne's management at a time when other golf clubs were failing.

The first Pro-Am Tournament, The Western Open, sponsored by Wadworth, was held in 1994. By 1995, there was a team of twelve working under Lord Shelburne on the various aspects of administration, along with a number of part-time employees. A Marketing Manager was recruited to develop the business. Nigel Blenkarne was appointed Director of Golf, while Head Green Keeper Duncan Bawcutt in 1996 managed a team of five and two part-time Youth Training Scheme workers.

At the beginning of 1995 the men's changing rooms were extended to double the size. A grand marquee with seating capacity for up to 200 was used on a seasonal basis for large parties and weddings, with a containerised kitchen in the west barn. That year the first wedding was celebrated at the Golf & Country Club.

Gill Cooper joined the Golf & Country Club team in 1996: today, twenty years later, as Hospitality and Revenue Manager, she manages a team of six. The Club, with a steady increase in membership, experienced a good year in 1996/97 with a total 24,500 rounds for 1995/6 and 23,500 rounds played by November 1996. At the same time, corporate and society days increased and the catering and bar services were doing well. The business was now producing an operating surplus – swallowed up, of course, by loan repayments. A three-year programme of some 10.5 miles of drainage improvements ensured that the course was playable during the winter months.

During 1992, Queenwood was extended and converted into a four-bedroomed golf lodge, with servicing and catering provided. The lodge was opened in 1993, its rooms beautifully furnished by Lady Shelburne with both modern and antique furniture and pictures. The occupancy rate increased steadily, with many return visits: the visitors' book entries admirably express how much the lodge and its comfortable and informal surroundings are appreciated. Clementina Mirylees was one of the first

Queenwood cook-housekeepers, from 1994 to 2002.

Queenwood Golf Lodge (Charles Leather)

Capital expenditure of £5m on the Golf & Country Club had far overrun estimates, and it had become necessary to help pay for the project by selling property and family possessions. Hangar Park Farm was put on the market in 1991, and in 1992 planning permission was obtained for 41 houses at Redhill.

In December 1992 the papers of Lansdowne ancestor Sir William Petty (1623–1687) were sold by private treaty to the British Library. This unique archive includes the Down Survey maps of Ireland: made under Petty's supervision, they are the first scientifically-measured maps of the country. Over the next three years there were sales of further groups of important political and literary papers, almost all of which are now in public collections: those of the 1st, 3rd and 5th Marquesses in the British Library; Admiral Lord Keith's papers at Greenwich; and those of his son-in-law, the Comte de Flahault, in the French *Archives nationales*. Depressing as it was to see these papers leave the family, there is benefit in knowing that they are now not only in safe keeping but also more easily accessed by scholars. They also provided the resources necessary to finance a viable future for Bowood.

Bowood's higher subscription in comparison with other Wiltshire course rates appeared to be no deterrent. The increase in corporate and social events by 1997 led to large block booking of the course resulting in a slight reduction in membership, although this could be partially alleviated by restricting the mornings to members only. There was, however, now no reason to delay implementation of the long-planned next phase of the Golf & Country Club, upon which construction work began in October 1997. Ferguson Mann's sympathetic design blends comfortably, in similar materials and style, with the existing clubhouse and ancillary buildings, still allowing the Listed buildings to dominate in principal views.

A new 11,000 sq.ft. single-storey complex was constructed between the clubhouse and the west barn, to form the Kerry Suite of conference/banqueting rooms and a brasserie. Sliding screens allow the largest interior space to be converted into two or three smaller rooms to suit events of different kinds and sizes. The entrance hall, facing north to the golf course, allows direct access to the Kerry Bar which looks on to an attractive internal courtyard with a fountain. The Kerry Bar provides space for hospitality as visitors gather for events – or simply a comfortable informal meeting place. Doors from the suite lead to the Brasserie conveniently adjacent to the clubhouse which is accessed via the glazed corridor constructed as a part of Phase I of the building work. The Brasserie is served by the clubhouse kitchen; and a new kitchen with preparation rooms was formed in the west barn. In its central position, the new kitchen would also serve the hotel planned for Phase III of the project. A Country Landowners Association Award was presented in 1998 on completion of the Home Farm buildings conversion.

The Kerry Suite, comfortably furnished and decorated to a high specification under the supervision of Lady Shelburne, was opened at the end of June 1998 by Ronnie Corbett.

Minor changes to the clubhouse had involved the conversion of the former ground floor dining and club rooms into offices. Together with the marquee, the Kerry Suite would now meet the high demand for conference and wedding facilities, providing 200 covers in the marquee, 165 in the Suite and 70 in the Brasserie. A necessary increase in staff, especially under new Catering Manager Tony Critchley, required 18 full-time and 48 part-time workers in all Golf & Country Club departments.

The Kerry Suite and Hotel, 2016

In August 1999 Bowood was host to the European Challenge Tour Championship, sponsored by Beazer Homes. In the same year Director of Golf Nigel Blenkarne left and was replaced by Max Taylor who stayed as Head Professional until 2006.

By 1990, almost all Estate departments were computerized. Roger Thorne took over as Financial Controller in 1991, remaining in post until December 2000. In 1993, the Estate Office was reorganized and a part-time accounts assistant was taken on to help with increased work generated by the Golf & Country Club until the appointment of a dedicated accountant in 1996. At the end of 1999 both John Wallis and

Philip Cubbon retired: Julian Sayers became Bowood Consulting Agent and Nick Bailey, Assistant Estate Manager.

By 1991, the Open Days business was the major gross income source for the Estate. It was estimated, however, that at least 150,000 visitors a year to Bowood were needed to cover running costs, and numbers had fallen below this target. Figures picked up in 1993 but poor weather that year and the next kept them at a lower level than in the 1980s. In 1994, it was considered that around 70 per cent of the 127,484 visitors were principally drawn by the adventure playground which continues to attract around 50,000 children each year to the present day.

Building the helter-skelter in the adventure playground

A £50 season ticket was introduced in 1995 (£45 purchased in advance). These were welcomed by local visitors, many of whom brought children to the adventure playground after school and during the holidays. Entry to the House and Gardens now cost £4.50 for adults (£4.10 for concessions) and £2.60 for children. Tickets for the rhododendrons were £2.50 or £1.50 if combined with an entry ticket to the House and Gardens.

On 8 August 1995, the Performing Arts Group orchestra played its first programme of popular classical music at Bowood with a grand finale firework and laser display. Six thousand tickets were sold, setting a trend for concerts in ensuing years. The 1996 Pro-Am Golf Tournament at Bowood allowed joint entry to that event and the House and Gardens, together attracting around 6,000 visitors in one day. A similar joint-entry event in 1997 and another popular Performing Arts Festival in August were major fine-weather attractions. There was an increase in other large events held in the park during the 1990s, including car enthusiasts' gatherings. Visitor numbers, always sensitive to weather conditions, were down to 115,445 in 1998, with 25 inches of rain during the seven-month open season, but they rose again in 1999.

Anna Blundell returned as House Administrator in 1995; she remained in post for another five years, when she and Catering Manager Lynne Rawlings both retired. Apart from Anna and her Assistant Jane Meadows, Lynne and full-time Head of Security Dick French, there were in 1995 some 54 part-time and seasonal staff employed in the Open Days business. During the summer of that year a weekend of events was held to celebrate the 20th anniversary of opening Bowood to the public under Lord Shelburne's custodianship. Also in commemoration of this anniversary, an updated edition of the Bowood Guidebook with many more images was produced.

The 1994 Sunday Trading Act had an immediate effect on garden centre shopping which had hitherto attracted customers unable to shop elsewhere. By then the Bowood Garden Centre was making a loss, largely owing to unsold stock at the end of each season. Hilliers Nurseries purchased a franchise for plant sales in 1995 but were unable to make a profit: the agreement was terminated and surplus stock sold off prior to closing on Christmas Eve. In 1996 the Garden Centre was stocked and maintained by a local wholesale company, with 25 per cent of the selling price retained by Bowood. Finally, in 1998 Whitehall Nurseries agreed to take on a franchise, placing Charlotte Hart, a member of their own staff in charge. The Garden Centre Gift Shop under Lady Shelburne's management continued to trade satisfactorily, with 1996 and 1997 bringing in good profits. Takings by the shop and Whitehall Nurseries, however, were inevitably affected by the weather and increased staff costs, and in 2000 it was decided to close down both enterprises and convert the Garden Centre building into a coffee shop.

Head Gardener Derek Duck retired in 1995, having served at Bowood with dedication and quiet distinction for 44 years. A team of four gardeners, including a number of new staff over the next few years, now cared for the terraces, Garden Centre, Golf & Country Club and the private walled gardens. Dougie Morse, who ran the Bowood Social Club for some years in Lord Shelburne's old aircraft hangar (now the Green Keepers' shed at The Osprey), worked as Acting Head Gardener when Derek retired; he moved to Dorset in 2002, after 37 years of service. Still working as a Bowood gardener, now with special responsibilities for the terrace gardens and security, is Stephen Starr, who joined the team in 1986.

The upper terrace in spring (Jarrold & Sons Ltd.)

Over the winter of 1995/6 the upper terrace planting was redesigned by Lady Mary Keen. The intention was to reflect more closely the 19th-century gardening style introduced by the 3rd Marquess, with annual plantings of successively flowering tulips among forget-me-nots, followed by pelargoniums interspersed with miniature roses. Box edging was added to each flower bed. Owing to wear on the paths between the beds, the grass was replaced with gravel. The scheme is now one of the special delights of the Bowood gardens during the open season. To celebrate the new planting scheme, an exhibition on the history of Bowood park and gardens was mounted in the orangery in 1996.

During the 1990s, the impact of storm damage was still evident and remedial work continued in the park and woodlands. Some of the fallen timber was used for seats in the 'Schoolroom' adjacent to the lavatories in the former apple store, where children on school visits could leave their coats and sandwiches or sit on rainy days. The cleanly cut section of the fallen *Cedrus atlantica*, showing its annual tree rings, was mounted on the Schoolroom wall.

The total cost of the clear-up was about £250,000; only £150,000 of this sum being covered by grants and timber sales. Wessex Woodland took on the marketing of estate timber from 1991: this was successful at first but the Forestry department, with only two full-time employees, was by 1998 running at an annual deficit. Head Groundsman David Cleverly received a long-service award in 1997, having worked with outstanding commitment and ability at Bowood for 50 years. He was to retire three years later.

In 1991, just over 1,460 acres of farmland were let out and there were then only two dairies which by 1993 were operated on contract farming agreements. Both dairies were updated in 1995, with Andrew Denley running Tossels and Steven Denley, Pinhills. In 1996 the dairies were amalgamated prior to construction of a single new dairy at Tossels in 1997. Andrew Denley terminated his contract in 1998, leaving Steven to continue on some 570 acres with a reduced herd of 250–300 cows.

1995 was a good year for sheep and cattle rearing, with sheep doing even better in 1996 owing to the BSE scare. The beef enterprise was closed down in 1997 and the sheep operation re-organised. Richard Keevil monitored the dairy operation for a further year and some staff redundancies were made, including Andrew Duck who had worked as Bowood shepherd since 1988. Bill Goddard and Keith Matthews were found alternative employment on the estate. The dairy was taken back in hand in 1999 but was closed in May 2000 and the land let for grazing and maize production. In 1998 the sheep flock was run on a 440-acre contract, with 15 per cent of the profit going to Bowood Farms, but the contract was terminated as unprofitable in 1999 and the grassland let.

The success of the Golf & Country Club had demonstrated that the decision largely to come out of farming had been a wise one, allowing the Estate to capitalise on rents without the unstable risks of the agriculture business.

Throughout the 1990s the Shoot was let, Bowood Keeper John Maynard being employed on a contracted-out basis and assisting with security within the wider park and woodland. Necessary deer culling took place on a limited scale. Fishing permits were sought annually: 55 for the Bowood Lake, including four junior rods, and 20 for the Calstone Reservoir syndicate.

By 1991, most of the estate properties had already been re-roofed with grant-aid for insulation. Of around 90 cottages, some 50 are Listed, which demands extra expense on repairs and improvements. Nevertheless, the overall cost of repairs had decreased by 1992 as more properties were now in better condition. In that year the restoration of Pinhills House was completed and work began on restoring 17th-century Laggus Farmhouse to create a single dwelling for Rupert and Lady Arabella Unwin and their family. Leases on the pubs at Derry Hill and Sandy Lane were due for renewal and the properties were renovated before being re-let. Stock Street Farm House also underwent major renovation in 1998/9 before being let to Lady Shelburne's mother, Lady Davies and, subsequently, to James and Lady Rachel Spickernell and their young family.

John Harrison, Estate Carpenter, retired in December 1997 after 28 years of highly skilled work at Bowood. There was now only a small estate maintenance team of two, mainly decorating between lettings and mowing grass at tenanted properties. Outside contractors were used for building, electrical and plumbing repairs and B.A.Vines Ltd. was relied upon for larger construction work. In 1995 Bowood House was rewired: a major project, including installation of a more efficient smoke alarm system.

As the millennium approached, significant events were to bring changes in the family, to Bowood and to the nearby village of Derry Hill and Studley.

Chapter eight

Changes at the turn of the millennium and the building of Bowood Hotel & Spa

The death of the 8th Marquis of Lansdowne on 25 August 1999 was not unexpected: aged 87, he had been in poor health for some years. Following retirement to Perthshire in 1972, he continued to support Lord Shelburne's efforts to make a success of the Wiltshire estate. Among his occupations in Scotland, Lord Lansdowne had been a keen fisherman and had also pursued his long held interest in Anglo-French relations. He was survived by his fourth wife, Penelope Bradford.

The funeral took place in the chapel at Bowood on 3 September. After the service, the coffin decked with Perthshire heather was placed on a refurbished 19th-century Bowood farm wagon and drawn by a magnificently caparisoned Wadworth dray horse through the park to the mausoleum, followed on foot by family and friends. Memorial services were held at St John's Kirk, Perth and St Margaret's, Westminster.

The Lansdowne title now passed to the present Marquis who gave his maiden speech, promoting organic farming, in the House of Lords on 22 October 1999. With his wide experience, notably in farming, local politics, business and public affairs over many years, he would have served the country well in Parliament but the 9th Marquis was one of many hereditary peers to lose their seats under the November 1999 House of Lords Act. Among his voluntary posts at around that time, Lord Lansdowne had been a founder English Heritage Commissioner from 1983 to 1989. He was Deputy President and then President of the Historic

Houses Association from 1986 to 1993; and President of South West Tourism from 1989, a position he continued to hold until 2006. He had also been President of the Wiltshire Historic Buildings Trust since 1994 (and remains in post to date). In addition to these offices, he was President of the Wiltshire Association of Boys Clubs and Youth Clubs from 1976. In 1990, he had been appointed a Deputy Lieutenant for Wiltshire and would become Vice-Lieutenant in 2012, retiring in February 2016. He had also served as a Prince's Council Member of the Duchy of Cornwall since 1990, a post he relinquished in 2001.

Closer to home, with an active interest in the well-being of the village, he was (and still is) a member of Calne Without Parish Council. In the wider local community, he had taken a leading role in the Calne Project, a charity set up to encourage the social, environmental and economic regeneration of Calne following closure of the Harris factory, a major town employer. Thus, a very busy working life was running in parallel with a number of demanding voluntary activities in the county and nationally. Such obligations were to continue with the added responsibilities of the marquessate.

Lord Robert Mercer Nairne, the 8th Marquis' younger son, inherited Meikleour House beside the River Tay, and its lowland estate. The hill land, known as the Tullybeagles Estate, had been given by Lord Lansdowne to Lord and Lady Shelburne as a wedding present in 1987: maintained as a rough shoot, its small lowland farm of around 350 acres covered running costs. The farm house, Berryhill, had been enlarged in 1990 to make room for regular family visits.

Among the titles inherited by Lord Lansdowne was the Irish Earldom of Kerry which was passed to Simon, his eldest son and heir, then aged 28. Lord Kerry, awarded a Cambridge BA Hons degree in Archaeology and Anthropology in 1992, was then undertaking a research project on the life of his distinguished ancestor, the 5th Marquess, culminating in a Doctorate of Philosophy from the University of East Anglia. Having also completed a course in business studies, he takes a close interest in the running of Bowood. The wedding of Simon to Nadine Mentior took place at Bowood in January 2016 and they now live in London.

Lord Lansdowne's younger daughter, Lady Rachel, had been the first of his children to marry: her wedding to James Spickernell took place in St Mary's Church, Calne in November 1991. Her elder sister Lady Arabella, having worked as Personal Assistant to Jasper Conran and then in fashion journalism, married Rupert Unwin in September 1993. She has continued to work part-time and is now (2016) Alumnae Relations Manager for St Mary's School, Calne. The Spickernells and Unwins live in houses on the Bowood Estate, where the young cousins could grow up near one another, some of them attending local schools.

Lord William, youngest of the Petty-Fitzmaurices, completed his schooling at Millfield and worked in a number of different jobs before his marriage to Rebecca Sansum in March 2004. They and their three daughters now live in Chippenham where William runs a local handyman business.

Lady Frances Shelburne, the children's mother, had always kept in close touch with her family. She died on 6 January 2004. After the Petty-Fitzmaurice children in her care had grown up, Nanny Cruttenden lived in retirement in Derry Hill.

The new Lady Lansdowne had moved her interior design business, Fiona Shelburne, to Bowood in 1995, where the Head Gardener's bothy in a corner of the walled garden was converted into her office. With Personal Assistant Helen Evelyn-Wood, she continues to undertake commissions for private clients in the UK and abroad to the present day.

A house the size of Bowood has a dedicated team of staff to look after its various needs as well as those of the family and visitors. Among the employees in the private house in recent years were Sarah Whiting who became part-time Housekeeper in September 1996 and Robert Mackie who was employed as Butler in 1998. Marnie Duncan took over as Housekeeper in 2004 and stayed until 2010 when she and her husband Danny returned home to St Helena. John Hudson has been the Lansdowne's Butler since November 2006; and Elizabeth Springett who joined the House staff in 2008 is now Housekeeper.

Fortunately, there were no death duties to be paid on the Bowood Estate, since it had been handed over to the 9th Marquis long before his father died and various trusts had been set up to avoid taxation.

Money was, of course, constantly needed to pay for the running of Bowood and for the enormous cost of financing each stage of the Golf & Country Club project which it was intended would eventually underwrite the solvency of the Estate. Funds were raised partly through sales of chattels owned by the Collection Trust set up by the 9th Marquis in 1974. Further finance was raised by selling outlying properties such as Stockley and Willowbrook Farms, along with estate land for new housing south of Calne at Wessington Park and Wenhill (1999–2003). Twenty small-to medium-sized commercial business units to let were created in three phases between 2000 and 2006 in former farm buildings at Forest Gate Farm, Pewsham.

Forest Gate Farm converted to offices (Charles Leather)

Lansdowne Crescent East and West, the first phase of housing development at Redhill, in Derry Hill and Studley village, had been built by the 8th Marquis in the 1960s. The intention always was to extend this development between the village and the A4 on land formerly used as allotments and small holdings and now with no practicable use for agriculture. In 1994, with plans for Golf Club expansion under way, thoughts were again turning to further development at Redhill.

Particular care was needed, since Derry Hill and Studley is still very much an estate village where many present and retired estate employees live. It was important that the gain from any new development should ensure some benefit in return to this rather exceptional community, including improvements to the village hall and provision of land for associated parking. In 1996, planning permission was gained for 28 houses, tied to the construction of a new village hall, parking area and access road, the Estate providing land for that purpose. It was hoped that a Millennium Fund grant might be obtained for building the new hall, along with a developer-funded contribution: unfortunately, however, the grant application was refused. In response, following sale of the housing land to a developer in 1997, the Estate offered, at a peppercorn rent, a 999-year lease on land for the hall, car park and all-weather sports pitch, and a 99-year lease on a plot of land known as Petty Acre for amenity open space. One third of the profit made on the sale in 1999 of the old village hall for residential use was donated to a new charitable Trust set up to build and maintain the new village hall; while further charitable donations included £225,000 from the Estate. New houses and the village hall were constructed over the period 2001–06. Retired Bowood Estate employees were some of the first occupiers of the low cost housing included in the mixture of dwelling types.

In 2008, the old Scout hut in Derry Hill was rebuilt in a new location. The land, like the Bowood Sports Ground, is leased by the Bowood Estate to Derry Hill and Studley village at a peppercorn rent.

Within a year of opening in 1998, the new Kerry Suite was attracting business and the Golf & Country Club had a well-established reputation as a premier venue in the region. The European Challenge Tour Championship, sponsored by Beazer Homes from 1999 to 2000, attracted welcome publicity for the course which, in the December 1999 edition

The Lansdowne Hall, Derry Hill village

New houses, Derry Hill village

of *Today's Golfer Magazine*, was chosen as seventh in the Top Ten of Category 2 Courses (those with a £20–£50 green fee); and was again nominated one of the UK Top Ten Courses in 2000. Despite exceptionally wet weather from August to October 2000, Bowood was one of the few Wiltshire courses that remained open. Overall bookings were up by 40 per cent in 2001 and the number of rounds played, up by 22 per cent. Catering Manager Tony Critchley had successfully built up the Kerry Suite business for conferences, weddings and social occasions. The quality and standard of the golf course had become outstanding under the care of Course Manager Ross Williams and his team of eight green keepers; and a very successful European Challenge Tour Championship was sponsored by Charles Church in July 2001. Andrew Doel followed Tania Coles as Head Accountant in 2002. By then, ten years after opening the Golf & Country Club, the annual turnover had increased twelvefold.

At the turn of the millennium, plans were already being considered for Phase III of the Golf & Country Club project: construction of an hotel and health spa to complement the facilities offered by the Kerry Suite, together with the addition of nine holes to the golf course. Unexpected opposition from English Heritage and the Garden History Society led to delays in seeking planning permission but outline consent was obtained in 2002 for a 149-bed hotel, along with permission for extension of the course. Architects Donald Insall Associates and the Street Design Partnership worked on scheme designs. The next task was to secure a suitable partner and sufficient finance to build and run the hotel.

By 2003, however, it had become clear that around two years of construction work on a large hotel, probably involving redevelopment of the Kerry Suite, would be enormously disruptive for the Golf & Country Club business, now pre-eminent in the region. This, together with problems encountered in negotiations with potential developers, resulted in the decision to aim for a much smaller hotel and spa reflecting Bowood's unique character. Over the next two years, through a market downturn and a major re-organisation of the Golf department, the focus was on running the present business and exploring options. Under new

Director of Golf John Hansel, the excellent reputation of the Golf Club was maintained although profits were down. Bookings for weddings, social functions, conferences and Queenwood Golf Lodge fell slightly in 2006 along with a weakening of the golf market. These trends pointed to the critical need to press ahead with the hotel project.

By late 2005 it was decided that the hotel would be developed without outside involvement and run by an in-house general manager and the proposed extension to the golf course would be abandoned. Planning permission was sought and finally secured in August 2006 for a 43-bedroom hotel and health spa, with extended consent for a further 20 bedrooms and conference facilities. There was strong demand for a smaller hotel which would dovetail well with conference facilities offered in the Kerry Suite during the week and still allow for short-stay golfers, wedding parties and weekend breaks for those seeking comfortable and attractive leisure facilities in beautiful surroundings.

Once again finance was a major consideration, with the rising Golf & Country Club turnover still leaving a deficit owing to running costs and the outstanding loan to be repaid. The continuing project would depend upon sales of property and development land, as already mentioned. Additional funding was secured through the important July 2004 sale at Sotheby's of Lord Lansdowne's *Portrait of Mrs Baldwin* by Sir Joshua Reynolds. Only half of the sale price of £3.4m could be invested in the hotel, however, as over 50 per cent of the sum was absorbed in commission fees and taxation. The portrait was originally purchased by the 3rd

Mrs Baldwin in Eastern Dress, portrait in oils by Sir J. Reynolds, 1782

Marquess but had no other Lansdowne family connection; it now hangs on public view in the Compton Verney Gallery, Worcestershire.

By 2008, when hotel construction costs had escalated, it was regrettably decided to sell Tullybeagles, the Lansdownes' much loved Scottish estate and buy a smaller, more practical holiday home in Devon.

In July 2006, James Stewart was appointed General Manager with responsibility for the Golf & Country Club business, visitor-related Open Days activities at the House and Gardens, and to work with Lord Lansdowne on development of the Hotel & Spa. Lord Lansdowne led the hotel design team from the start. Consultant François Nairác was appointed to co-ordinate the development scheme alongside architects Aukett Fitzroy Robinson, with the aim of starting construction in August 2007. In the event, the chosen developer John Sisk & Son began work on the building in November 2007 at a fixed price.

Construction work, screened by hoardings, had some effect on Golf & Country Club bookings although turnover was marginally up overall in 2008. An expensive annual programme of repairs to the 16-year-old golf course was begun in 2009 and, in the same year, Queenwood Golf Lodge was refurbished.

Hotel building progress was, however, hampered by architects Purcell Miller Tritton's difficulties in keeping up with the demands of the contractors and consultants, leading to delays and additional costs. Perhaps in part owing to these conflicting pressures and following an operation for a blocked carotid artery in 2007, Lord Lansdowne underwent triple bypass surgery in early 2008, followed by a necessary period of convalescence. By December 2008, a renegotiated sum was agreed for project completion and opening in May 2009.

The new 32,000 sq.ft. complex, just west of the Golf & Country Club, occupies the site of former Home Farm buildings. Incorporating earlier Listed stone walling around the entrance court, it is principally new-build, in a style reflecting the 19th-century Italianate Golden Gates entrance at Derry Hill. The rendered outside walls are softening in colour over time and as climbing plants are becoming established. The car parks and biomass boiler are located in woodland close by, on the exit route to the A342.

Entrance to Bowood Hotel, 2016

The stunning design work by Lady Lansdowne has resulted in the creation of a contemporary hotel interior with a marked historic house feel. Light-coloured walls complement antique and modern furnishings with a strong emphasis on relaxation and comfort. There are links to Bowood and the Lansdownes throughout: the furniture, portraits and paintings giving a strong sense of belonging to the Estate.

The hotel entrance hall leads to the bar, restaurant and library on the ground floor, each with widows looking out over the park and golf academy course. There are comfortable chairs before an open fire in the library, dominated by the gaze of the 5th Marquess, whose original portrait hangs over the chimneypiece. With fine Perthshire landscapes on three of its walls, the library's fourth wall is filled with books from Bowood House. The nearby bar is hung with Lansdowne political caricatures and a modern bust of the 1st Marquess stands on the counter.

Bowood Hotel, Spa & Golf Course from the air (Arabella Unwin, May 2013)

The kitchen, housed in the west barn of the original farmyard complex, serves on one side the hotel restaurant and on the other, the Kerry Suite. A corridor from the hotel entrance hall leads to 43 luxury en-suite bedrooms on three floors. There are six larger suites named after Lansdowne family members, enhanced by historically-themed photographic studies by Peter Lavery whose striking work also appears elsewhere in the building.

The spa is approached direct from the entrance court for non-resident members but may also be reached from the hotel. Again, the decorative scheme is light and modern and based on comfort and tranquillity. The glass-fronted gym, overseen by trained fitness staff, and a breathtaking infinity pool both look south to the golf academy course and lake. There are shower rooms, a steam room, Jacuzzi, rock sauna and hot tub, and a small café-bar with an outside terrace seating area.

Among the Bowood staff who helped to bring the final stages of the project together was James Stewart, who had maintained firm control over progress and completion. The interior work was co-ordinated by

Bowood Hotel: the library

Bowood Spa: the infinity pool

Viktoria Kowal who was instrumental in ensuring that various building design problems were resolved. Resident Estate Manager Charles Leather oversaw the construction of the drainage and sewerage systems, a biomass heating system to be fired with estate wood chippings (one of the first of its kind in the country), and the landscaping around the hotel including the ha-ha along the southern front and the entrance court to the north. The Bowood Garden Team, under Garden Designer Rosie Abel-Smith's direction, put the professional finishing touches to these landscaped areas. A splendid dinner was given for all of those involved in construction work a few days before the new Hotel & Spa were opened on 16 May 2009 by the Duchess of Cornwall.

Now known as the Bowood Hotel, Spa & Golf Resort, the c.56,000 sq.ft. development, conceived more than 20 years earlier, was completed shortly after the collapse of Lehmann Brothers and the onset of a major global recession. Reductions in corporate golf activities led to declines in profit across the business, resulting in a drop in turnover of just over a quarter of a million pounds in 2009. It had become the most challenging period in the country house hotel industry and by 2010 it seemed likely that it would be another three years or so before hotel trading would reach maturity.

The unexpected loss of key staff members, including James Stewart and Accountant Andrew Doel in early 2010 brought additional worries, but Bowood Enterprises Financial Controller Nick Hemmings and Charles Leather stepped into the breach, managing the day-to-day finances and the green keeping department, respectively. Lord Lansdowne took over the management of the business for five months, maintaining weekly meetings with departmental heads, until a new General Manager was appointed.

Despite setbacks, the new Hotel & Spa business began to grow, bolstered by faith in its potential and the determination of its managers and staff. By 2010, there were 29 full-time and eight part-time staff, with three casual employees and the Hotel & Spa were getting excellent ratings on TripAdvisor: an immediate indicator of good – or indeed bad – service and value for money.

During the winter of 2009–10, a spa treatment room was created in the hotel tower, its decoration and fitting-out overseen by Lady Lansdowne. The facility has proved very successful, with sufficient demand for expansion to a suite of treatment rooms when funding becomes available.

In 2011 Christoph Brooke, Managing Director of Hillbrook Hotels, took over the general management of the Hotel & Golf Resort for a year with staff employed by Bowood. Running the business had become extremely challenging and some cost-savings on staff were necessary. The new team included Finance Manager Helen Baker, and Course Manager Jaey Goodchild. The need to secure customers at the right price for the range of facilities offered requires a skilled marketing team along with daily co-ordination and data-exchange between departments. Some 80 per cent of the business was now being captured via the internet, with the main emphases on leisure, golf and weddings during the summer months, and on corporate business and spa breaks along with Christmas and New Year party nights during the winter.

By mid 2012, however, with the loss of valued staff such as Karen and Chris Dawson, it had become obvious that the business would benefit from a full-time senior manager on-site. Charles Morgan was appointed General Manager in October and, together with his newly-appointed Personal Assistant and Human Resources Administrator Jennifer Lamercraft, began to stabilize the situation. Although total revenue had increased by 14 per cent under Hillbrook Hotels, direct costs had increased, leading to an overall loss. Efficiencies were implemented, notably in the four separate catering outlets, and course management expenses were reduced. Although Golf Club membership had fallen, Spa membership was strong and the hotel occupancy hovered at around 68 per cent over the year, its popularity in part owing to immaculate housekeeping supervised by Corinne Weaver.

A new 500kw replacement biomass boiler was installed in August 2012 under the direction of Charles Leather who, together with Nick Hemmings, continued to keep an overall professional eye on relevant aspects of the business.

The 2013/14 financial year brought a 5.9 per cent increase in revenue. All heads of departments attended training courses and dependence on unskilled staff was minimized by offering suitable part-time and permanent posts, generating security and loyalty. A new Business Development Manager helped to achieve outstanding reviews on TripAdviser by 2013. There are now (in 2016) two Marketing and Development Managers, one for the Hotel, Spa & Golf Resort and one for the Bowood House and Grounds Open Days business. Bookings for the Hotel & Spa were up in 2015 but use of the function rooms and the golf course had gone down: a constantly changing situation, indicative of the complex and sensitive nature of the industry.

While the development and running of the Bowood Hotel, Spa & Golf Resort had taken up much staff time over the past ten years or so, activities elsewhere on the estate continued in parallel, with closer links being developed between the different enterprises they embraced.

Chapter nine

The continual need for new attractions

There were a number of changes of personnel in the Estate Office at the turn of the millennium, some already mentioned. Sarah True was appointed Estate Manager at the end of 2001. In the same year Amy Ryan became her Administrative Assistant managing the mainly short-term property lettings, for which the Estate was gaining an excellent reputation. It was clearly more satisfactory, from both financial and practical points of view, not to use a commercial estate agency for this task.

Charles Leather took over from Sarah as Assistant Estate Manager in 2004 and remains in post as Resident Estate Manager today, his own workload increasing as the Bowood enterprises have expanded. Sarah Goodall became Charles' Assistant in 2008 and continues to work part-time; while local farmer Nigel Cole now acts as Farm and Building Consultant.

Networking of the office computers and the installation of a computerised property management system were completed by 2002 and in 2008 Nick Hemmings, took on what had become a highly demanding post as Financial Controller of all the various Bowood enterprises. Val Morrison, Lisa Newton and Geraldine Humphries have given long service as part-time Accounts Assistants, the last still in post.

Estate Office Receptionist Shirley Bennett, who joined Bowood in 1989, job-shared in her later years of employment; and in 2007 Office/IT Administrator Mary Weston took over the work full-time until 2012. Blue Sky Computing Ltd. has been employed for many years as IT consultants for all of the Bowood enterprises, computers now forming a vital management tool.

Beverley Gould, appointed House Administrator in November 1999, was followed by Christine Fitt in 2003 with the changed job title of Visitor Manager; with two new posts for a marketing manager and hospitality co-ordinator being created.

Visitor numbers dropped below 120,000 in 2000, primarily owing to poor weather, but better weather in the following two years saw a rise to 154,458 by 2002. In 2000, surveys showed that no more than 5.7 per cent of visitors came from outside the United Kingdom, while around 11,000 under-fives came at no charge. Season ticket holders increased steadily, further indicating that focus on the local market would be crucial to the future of the business.

The Garden Centre building, originally costing £300,000 to build, was converted into the Temple Gate Coffee Shop for around £200,000: its opening in 2001 led to higher sales in the House Gift Shop where Jean Dupre's beautiful photographs of Bowood were sold as cards. In this year – and again in 2011 – the Calne Artists Group mounted displays in the orangery, strengthening links with the local community. The work of professional artists inspired by Bowood themes was of great interest to visitors.

The party tea rooms in the bothy, 2016

With emphasis on local repeat visits, an indoor soft play marquee, not dependent upon weather conditions, was installed for opening in the 2002 season beside the former bothy Garden Tea Room which was converted over the winter to incorporate two children's party rooms with pirate and fairy themes. These new activities grew in popularity over succeeding years.

In 2003 Bowood came 8th in the Historic Houses Association list of top visitor attractions, principally owing to the undiminished appeal of the adventure playground, along with another major outdoor concert and a Honda Family Day. Additional events in 2004 included a *Crimestoppers* show which alone attracted 16,000 people.

2004 was the 250th anniversary year of the Lansdownes' ownership of Bowood and a celebration weekend was arranged with an Indian theme. A disco dance was held in a marquee in front of the terraces for the family, friends and current and retired staff, and on the following night there was a private ball attended by the Prince of Wales.

The adventure playground today

Lady Arabella Unwin began organizing major events in 2005, raising some £73,000 that year in facility fees. It was estimated that up to 58,000 children used the adventure playground in 2005, many more than the usual 45–50,000. Claire Snape was appointed Visitor Manager in 2006 and remained in post until 2010; while Lynne Rawlings returned in 2006 as Catering Manager on a seasonal basis, following the departure of James Daniells.

Over the next few years, visitor numbers fluctuated, depending on the weather. Golf & Country Club General Manger James Stewart, responsible for integrating the two parts of the Bowood Enterprises where practicable, brought improvements in the business overall, with the help of Marketing Consultant Kerrie Leather. Charlotte Doherty, Marketing Consultant from 2007 onwards, has boosted national and international publicity for Bowood, promoting linked visits and special events, including day-time talks and activities at the Hotel, exclusive House and Garden tours for hotel visitors, and the Bowood orangery exhibitions.

Revenue from facility fees in 2007 amounted to £137,000, with an estimated £45,000 generated by event activities, including the summer concert in the park. These major events not only advertised Bowood but also allowed promotion to a wider audience of all that Bowood has to offer. In 2008, however, poor weather seriously affected trading at special events and led to low ticket sales resulting in cancellation of the last concert in the park. The cost of insurance had become very high, the recession was looming and major events of this kind were no longer financially viable.

The onset of the recession in 2009 resulted in a reduction in special events. The first Bowood Dog Show, run by Lady Lansdowne aided by volunteers, was held to raise money for local charities. Despite the recession, there was a rise in visitor-numbers, along with increases in coach bookings and season ticket sales: people were feeling the pinch and staying nearer to home for leisure activities.

This situation continued into 2010 when the only special events were the Charity Dog Show and the Wiltshire Game and Country Fair. It was now obvious that the recession, along with poor weather, was limiting the potential for revenue from hosting major events. In spite of higher season tickets sales, catering suffered as visitors needed to save on expenditure. Entry prices to Bowood were similar to those of competing properties but the average spend was £7.21 per head and a further 60p per head would be needed to break even.

Bowood Game Fair, aerial view from the east (Dominic Cross, 2015)

An increased marketing drive for 2011 included more feature-activities devised for children on celebration holidays, such as Easter and Halloween, by new Visitor Manager Katrina Drewitt. Catering menus were revised and, with the development of guided tour packages promoting the House, Gardens and Rhododendrons, visitor-numbers rose again that year and average spend increased to £7.69. There were three special events in the park which raised a total income of £36,600. The Charity Dog Show, however, was poorly attended owing to disastrous weather. With rainfall 11.23ins above a 10-year average in 2012, visitor-numbers fell to below 100,000 and the effects were felt throughout the business. Special events that year included the combined Charity Dog and Tractor Ted Farm Shows, generating over £33,000 for Wiltshire charities; the Living Heritage Country Fair; a corporate family fun day in August and the first Event Logic Duathlon in the autumn.

The success of the Tractor Ted Farm Show led to the introduction of Tractor Ted's Little Farm at Bowood in 2013. Tractor Ted children's story-book author Alexandra Heard, together with farmer David Horler have developed the now internationally successful Tractor Ted business, with a range of related products for young children, including DVD films, books, toys and clothing. The Little Farm at Bowood, commercially linked to the Tractor Ted business, is one of two farms promoting Tractor Ted in the UK. A wooden stable building was constructed close to the Café to house a range of farm animals for children to see, feed and pet. Miniature tractors and diggers were provided to play on and, in 2014, two mini-excavators. The farm was extended for the 2016 open season.

There were unexpected changes in Open Days staffing during 2013 and 2014 which led to service problems in catering and management. Assistant Visitor Manager Philip Barber took over and stabilized the situation in 2014 with the help of a part-time assistant. Lady Landsdowne ran the Bowood Restaurant with Nicky Thomas for a few weeks and has retained overall management of the Bowood Restaurant since then.

With the help of Curator Jo Johnston, the Bath Botanical Artists created an orangery exhibition for 2013 entitled 'Bowood's Botanical Heritage' and, in 2014, Jo prepared a thoughtful and interesting exhibition to commemorate the part played by Bowood and its family and staff during the First World War.

In 2014, Bowood received the prestigious Garden of the Year Award sponsored by the Historic Houses Association and Christie's. Visitor numbers had begun to rise again, while private garden tours raised £26,000: £9,000 higher than in the previous year. Charity and Event Logic sports days were held once more, along with other commercial events in the park, including a private dinner followed by fireworks. During the closed season, the Temple Gate Coffee Shop was refurbished and re-named the Tree House Café.

Tree House Café

By 2015, the Open Days department was employing 76 part- and full-time staff, including gardeners and groundsmen. Despite some increase in visitor numbers over the previous year, the business still made a loss and a dedicated marketing and development manager has now been employed to improve the situation. Events in the park included Toby Buckland's Garden Festival and the last Bowood Charity Dog Show. Since 2009 the Dog Show had raised nearly £300,000 for local charities supported by Lord and Lady Lansdowne, including the Wiltshire Blind Association, Dorothy House hospice, Youth Action Wiltshire and Community First. Two programmes of the *Antiques Roadshow* were filmed at Bowood on fine summer days in 2015 and shown in January 2016.

Since the turn of the millennium, and the employment in 2006 of David Glass as full-time Head Gardener and Garden Consultant Rosie Abel-Smith, the Bowood Gardens have been greatly improved and expanded. Each member of the team of four gardeners has his own area to care for in addition to dealing with the regular tasks of mowing, hedge cutting and so on. Stephen Starr looks after the terraces, David Powney maintains the vegetable garden and Rob Waller is responsible for the remainder of the private garden. David Glass assists where necessary, aided by Rosie one day a week. Over the winter of 2008/09, a new long border was created below the east terrace retaining wall: now maturing well, its spectacular planting gives colour throughout the open season.

The east terrace border (Anna Stowe, 2015)

The four-acre walled garden has slowly been brought back into full cultivation, so that it may be opened to the public for special tours. A decorative but practical half-acre vegetable garden which now supplies the Bowood restaurants as well as the private house, was created over some years, and a wild flower meadow was introduced alongside it in 2013. The picking border in the northeast quadrant, for flower arrangements in the house, was extended and improved and, during the following winters new borders were made on two further sides of the same quadrant, the meadow between them being home to hens and ducks.

In the southeast quadrant, nearest the house, are the swimming pool, soft fruit cage, fruit trees and a long border with a path bounded on the west side by a fine early 20th-century wistaria pergola. The only changes here since 1972 are the conversion of the tennis court into a croquet lawn and the replacement of old fruit trees. The massed plantings beneath the apple trees of tulips from previous seasons' terrace displays make an enchanting kaleidoscope of colour in spring.

The walled garden (Anna Stowe, 2015)

The northwest quadrant of the garden, with its long walk bordered by old fashioned roses, contains the greenhouses and cold frames for the propagation and care of houseplants and annuals. Here also, under glass, is the Bowood Muscat grape, originally developed at Bowood by 19th-century Head Gardener John Spencer. The garden restoration work here included mason Phil Slade's skilled repairs to steps and balustrading.

The 2014 Garden of the Year Award was the ultimate accolade for the efforts that have gone into making a visit to the Bowood gardens and pleasure grounds such an interesting and rewarding experience. It is hardly surprising that the garden tours led by David Glass and other knowledgeable Bowood guides are usually fully booked.

Geoff Partridge, a long-serving Bowood employee, took over from David Cleverly in 1999 as Head Groundsman. Steve Parfitt who has also worked on the estate for many years, is one of his team. In addition to mowing the parkland areas around the house and lake and in the pleasure grounds, the four groundsmen are responsible for the care of the trees and shrubs in all of these areas. The year-round programme of felling, trimming, new planting and maintenance over some 100 acres open to the public is exacting and carried out to a very high standard. New Bowood enterprises, such as the creation of a children's nature trail in 2006, the 2012 Jubilee Garden extension to the rhododendron gardens, and building Tractor Ted's Little Farm, along with annual tasks such as putting up and taking down notices at the beginning and end of each open season, all involve their dedicated input. Geoff's knowledge of the Bowood trees and shrubs is exhaustive and he ensures that the *Guide to Bowood Trees and Shrubs*, revised by Dr Owen Johnson in 2006 and produced in-house, is kept up to date.

Among the most exciting of the newly-established trees in the pleasure grounds is a Wollemi pine, planted at Bowood in 2008 and one of the first to be grown in the United Kingdom. Known only as a millions-of-years-old fossil until it was discovered in Australia in 1994, the species is classed as critically endangered.

Following the retirement of Head Forester Barry Lawrence in 2001, the timber business, involving some 750 acres and including some ancient woodland, has been managed under franchise to Wessex Woodland and, until the introduction of the Hotel & Spa biomass boiler, ran at a loss for the Estate. The Head Forester currently in post is Alan Day who is retained by the Estate; he and his assistant Dave Sanchez deal with minor felling and the supply of wood chippings for the boiler. They also help with projects such as the 2012 Jubilee Plantation close to Buck Hill Gate, created with an enabling grant for planting and maintenance to commemorate the Queen's Jubilee. The mainly fast-growing trees, such as plane, alder and poplar, will help to feed the biomass boiler. In time, there will be a combustion process to allow the boiler to produce electricity via a steam turbine which will help considerably to reduce the annual hotel lighting bill, currently over £140,000. Each year some 1,000 tons of wood for the boiler is supplied entirely from the estate: the wood is chipped and stored in the covered yard at The Waste. The Bowood sawmill is still operated to cut Bowood oak planking which is stored outside in the fresh air before being used for all estate repairs. Any surplus chippings and sawdust are used as soil improver.

In August 2011 Pond Tail Lake was dredged, the mud being spread over an arable field nearby. Designed as a silt pond by 'Capability' Brown, and crossed by a fine 18th-century stone bridge, this c.1.5-acre stretch of water at the southern entrance to the park helps to prevent silting-up of Bowood Lake.

Long stretches of the ten miles of estate roads were repaired or reconstructed in the same year, at a cost of £38,620, as part of a programme of maintenance costing an average £30,000–£40,000 a year. Problems have arisen as the result of modern surfaces having been laid over earlier tracks with insufficient foundations, particularly noticeable on the entrance road to the House and Gardens and where roads are now used by heavy agricultural and plant machinery.

The Bowood shoot and fishing have generally been let to syndicates, and in some cases fishing rods to individuals, including four junior rods, since the beginning of the 21st century. Tim Kamei is the present Gamekeeper with associated security duties in the park and woodlands.

The 570-acre Bowood dairy farm was closed in 2000 owing to falling milk prices and the need for substantial capital investment. The herd and dead stock were sold in May that year. As recorded earlier, a proportion of the milk quota was sold to a tenant farmer and the remainder let until its sale in 2001. A small sheep flock was managed on behalf of the Lansdownes by Christopher Farnsworth but it was slaughtered in 2001 owing to suspected Foot and Mouth Disease. The flock was not reinstated, to avoid complications over public access to the estate, and the grazing was let in 2002. Recently, however, a Bowood flock of 450 ewes has been introduced to graze the 500 acres of parkland in hand.

Stockley and Willowbrook Farms were sold in 2001 to the owners of the farm houses, leaving Bowood with no farm employees and all of its farmland now let. The Bowood Farm Business lettings were rationalized in 2003 to produce mostly larger blocks of land for local farmers to rent for longer periods, ensuring a better standard of land management and a secure income, the surplus from which is ploughed back into the Estate. Farm business tenancies now rent 1,485 acres, while 487 acres are let for short term grazing. Some farm buildings are also let on short term leases. This arrangement of long and short term farm business lettings and licenses still continues at a profit.

Proposals for a new garden centre to be built at Blounts Court, north of the A4 at Derry Hill and Studley, were considered over some years. It was hoped to include a roundabout on the A4 in the proposals to improve road crossing safety. Planning permission was secured and partially implemented in 2009 but with the doubtful viability of a small garden centre, housing appeared a more appropriate future for the site. Permission was granted in December 2013 for 28 houses, including 30 per cent affordable homes and an A4 pedestrian crossing. A second phase of 25 dwellings will be built to the west of these 28 houses.

Until 2004, B.A.Vines Ltd. undertook major repairs to estate buildings involving construction work; other contractors were used as appropriate, along with self-employed craftsmen, painters and decorators. After 2004, when the cost of using outside contractors had risen substantially, building repairs were carried out under the supervision of the Assistant Estate Manager with the advice of Nigel Cole where necessary, and using the professional skills of self-employed builders and carpenters, including builder and stone mason Phil Slade, and carpenter-joiners Andy Phelps, Chris Court and Ian Hillier. Considerable savings and a higher standard of workmanship were achieved in this way. Electrical work is undertaken by Wilts Electrical Contracting Ltd., run by Tony Matthews who was brought up on the Bowood Estate.

Repairs were undertaken in 2008 to the roof of the Golden Gates entrance to the park, a former lodge building now occupied by Golf &

Country Club employees.

Following partial collapse of the stallion box, a folly on the east side of the lake, in February 2010, rebuilding was undertaken with the advice of Nigel Cole. The work was finely executed by Phil Slade with Ian Hillier and Chris Court working on the timber structure.

The on-going five-year rolling programme of estate cottage and building repairs and refurbishment continues as necessary, although almost all estate property is now in excellent condition. Studley Lodge and Buckhill House were renovated in 2013 prior to letting.

19th-century estate cottages at Derry Hill, 2016

Two cottages in Derry Hill were refurbished after they became vacant in 2012: that at 41 Church Road having been lived in for 66 years by Mrs Angel, who died aged 103. Modernisation of two houses at the Black Dog entrance to Bowood will begin shortly, following the move of long-term tenant Mrs Holman to more comfortable accommodation in Derry Hill.

Mrs Angel and Mrs Holman both form links back to the time of the 5th Marquess who died in 1927.

Maintenance works include, of course, those to Bowood House itself, which constantly needs minor repairs owing to leaks, broken window panes and so on. Larger jobs include repairs to leadwork and roofs; and, in 2006, a number of floors and ceilings in the house were made sound following a serious leak from a water storage tank. Clock Tower repairs in 2013 included renewal of the weathervane, beautifully carved by Ian Hillier.

Rebuilding the north wing of the Estate Office
after the fire, 2015 (Jo Johnston)

Overnight on 27 October 2014, a fire broke out in the roof of the Estate Office owing to an outside main electric cable fault. Despite containment of the fire by the fire brigade, all of the rooms and their contents in the north range of the courtyard, including the reception area, conference room and recent archives room, were badly damaged or destroyed, as were some modern and older estate records and maps. Some archive material had been partially protected by huge flaps of fallen ceiling plaster or by being shelved in cupboards, only to suffer water damage in dousing the fire. All salvaged material was removed to storage in garages in the stable courtyard and Jo Johnston spent many months drying and labelling the papers and files that had been rescued. A novel and effective drying area was found in an empty greenhouse in the walled garden. Some paper conservation work was undertaken by specialists.

Fortunately, it was possible to find space in undamaged parts of the Estate Office where staff could double-up for nearly a year until they were able to return to the beautifully rebuilt and refurbished offices. One of the benefits of modern technology has meant that key modern estate records are held on computer, thus avoiding the loss of much vital information. Permanent losses of paper archive material, such as older staff records and records of property sales and purchases from the days before computers are, sadly, irretrievable.

Chapter ten

Change and innovation: past achievements and future prospects

The success that Bowood has become could hardly have been imagined when the young Lord Shelburne took over in 1972. He had determined at the outset not only to keep Bowood as a family home but also to safeguard the future of the house, the Bowood Collection, and the surrounding gardens and park for other people to enjoy. The task has demanded almost all of his time over the last 44 years, along with enormous responsibilities at work and in the wider community, His strong sense of tradition, coupled with an unwavering vision, good specialist advice and astute business skills gained in practice, have led to a highly worthwhile outcome. Lord Lansdowne is the first to admit, however, that he could not have achieved so much without the unfailing and practical support of his wife and the dedicated help of present and retired staff.

As the foregoing chapters have shown, opening to the public is a risky business, governed principally by the weather, notably unreliable in the UK, and by the changing social and political trends which influence market forces. This predictable unpredictability is clearly evidenced by the sometimes extreme variation in annual visitor figures, including the 1986 peak of 179,000 and a low of just over 90,000 in 2012.

The adventure playground was a master stroke at a time when such attractions were rare at historic properties; indeed it could be said that Bowood still leads the field for the quality and variety its adventure playground offers. It has consistently brought some 50,000 children as well as their families each year and now gives pleasure to a third generation since it was introduced in 1978. Without this facility, it is estimated that the house and grounds might attract no more than 30,000 visitors a year, whereas today's average is around 120,000.

Bowood lake from the arboretum

Within a few years of opening, the attractions for visitors to Bowood had been considerably expanded. The period coincided with a surge of interest in visiting country houses and the pursuit of leisure activities close to home, before cheap holidays abroad were more widely available. Visitor numbers then reached their highest. At the same time, farming was in decline: a matter of crucial significance for the landed estates that had survived the War and had made the most of what the Common Agricultural Policy offered. Despite high visitor figures, it was evident that opening alone would not keep the Estate afloat and, as farming income was falling, a long-term vision was conceived that would generate sufficient resources to ensure a viable future.

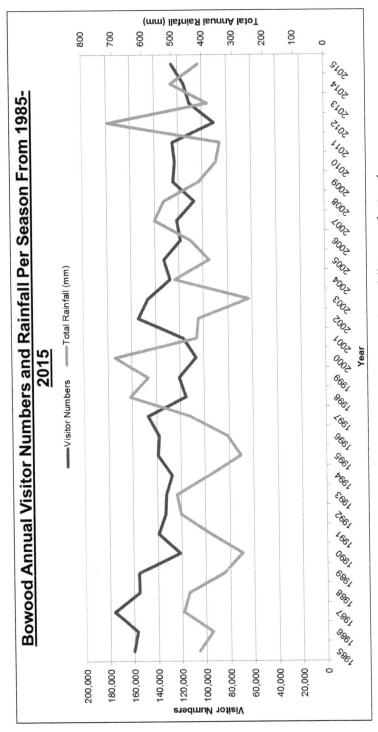

Graph showing annual visitor numbers and rainfall in mm during the open season (April to October inclusive) (Rose Johnston)

The parkland around the Home Farm provided the perfect opportunity to diversify into a golf course at the time when the game was becoming ever more popular. The long-term aim of the golf course and clubhouse, with conference facilities, hotel and spa alongside, was secured with outline planning consent in 1989. The project was developed in stages over 20 years, as finance could be raised and markets proved favourable. The overall aim was for the business to support the less profitable heritage properties and it is currently set on course to do so as substantial loans are gradually repaid. Lord Lansdowne was fast off the draw in starting the project at a time when it was easier to create a golf course and related facilities within a Grade I Listed park. Throughout the project, his finger was on the pulse, alongside architects and specialists, managing and making decisions on every detail and ensuring a uniformly high standard of presentation. The entire Bowood Estate business is extraordinarily complicated to run, owing to the interdependence of the facilities offered and its reliance on footfall. The use of computers has been and continues to be crucial to almost all of the Bowood Enterprises.

Farmland tenancies now bring in a reliable income, as does the letting of refurbished estate cottages, farm houses and business units formed in redundant farm buildings. The forestry business, owing to diversification into biomass energy, no longer runs at a loss. The woodlands have always been of special interest to Lord Lansdowne. Over a million trees have been planted since 1972, including oak, beech and pine in the woodlands and specimen trees in the pleasure grounds and park. The rhododendron gardens have been revitalized and extended. Some of the cut timber can be used for building repairs; and wood chippings are used to provide electricity to the Hotel & Spa complex through biomass energy – a technique likely to be even more profitable in future.

In order to achieve the major projects undertaken at Bowood, finance was raised by building houses and selling real estate with planning consent. In the early days, however, some art works and historic documents were sold but it is pleasing that the most important of them are now shown or available to see elsewhere in public collections and archives.

Nevertheless, they are all considered sad losses that were necessary to keep the remaining elements of Bowood and its Collection together.

The rhododendron gardens c.1979 (Sir Geoffrey Shakerley)

It has not all been a matter of losses, however. From time to time, Lord Lansdowne has purchased, privately or at auction, paintings and other works of art, such as the outstanding group of watercolours hanging in the exhibition rooms, the Cyrus tapestries in the sculpture gallery and paintings by Stanfield in the orangery, now considered pre-eminently important in their own right. In 2011, the magnificent portrait of the 1st Marquess by Jean-Laurent Mosnier was acquired to hang in the same room as another purchase, a portrait of the 2nd Marquess by Gainsborough. Such acquisitions were made with the express intention of enhancing Bowood and its collection. More rarely, real estate property has been purchased, such as Pitters Farm House with 65 acres, on the west side of Bowood Estate, bought in 2013 and now re-furbished and let as a family home.

The running of Bowood as a whole is especially complicated owing to the Settled Land Act under which Trusts were set up by the 5th Marquess leaving the majority of the Estate land in trust and severely restricting what Trustees, heirs and beneficiaries could do with it. In 1972 the 8th Marquis re-adjusted these Trusts into three independent Trust land holdings run by Trustees and a fourth owned by the present Lord Lansdowne outright. Income generated by each Trust remains within that Trust so that the businesses Lord Lansdowne has created have to meet the restrictive requirements of the relevant Trust in order to raise the revenue to maintain the whole. The Hotel, Spa & Golf Resort, for example, is built on Trust land leased to the business by its Trustees; while Bowood House and Gardens are owned by another Trust. Each Trust is taxed on its income and what is generated by Lord Lansdowne's businesses is taxed again on his income.

Further complications have arisen with the Bowood Collection Trust set up by the 9th Marquis in 1974 when he was inexperienced in legal matters. He was advised to set very restrictive terms on the long-term management of those important works of art owned by him which he then transferred into the Bowood Collection Trust to safeguard them for the future. The Trust's restrictions have in practice proved troublesome owing to the unpredictability of circumstances over the course of time. Occasionally, Trust possessions have had to be sold to help finance loans for major Bowood projects. But there are restrictions on sales of Trust chattels for which the Trustees have to be reimbursed – either financially or by exchanging them for chattels of equivalent value owned personally by Lord Lansdowne. Thus, alongside sales of real estate and a few valuable chattels of his own on the open market, it has been necessary for Lord

Lansdowne to exercise a financial juggling act over many years with the aim of retaining important family possessions at Bowood that are crucial to the integrity of the house and its display to the public.

Most of the items on show to the public are now in the Bowood Collection and are Conditionally Exempt from taxation. Some are specified as pre-eminent in their own right; others, for their significance as a group. Subject to ensuring the required conditions of care and display to the public, they are exempt from death duties.

The restriction of Sideways Tax Relief in 2013 has had a devastating effect on business. Hitherto, annual losses of opening Bowood to the public could be offset against revenue from other sources. This measure, introduced by Government without due consideration for its consequences, could jeopardise the futures of many important heritage properties in the United Kingdom. It will inevitably lead to further sales, including family treasures, to enable businesses to stay afloat. The private sector heritage is now under real threat, unlike that of historic properties owned by English Heritage and the National Trust which enjoy tax exemption as charities.

Value Added Tax levied on repairs to Listed buildings is another burden for owners of historic properties: it seems an unjust anomaly, since public benefit is involved.

The visiting public are hugely appreciative of what heritage properties such as Bowood offer and have an insatiable fascination for the country house life of the past and present, the family and servants: something that a National Trust or publicly-owned property can rarely provide with the same intimacy and immediacy of association. Most of us feel a positive affinity with the past and a visit to a country house and garden nowadays fosters that connection and allows it to be enjoyed for the best that it can offer, rather than the worst in terms of recollection of historic deprivations and present-day inequalities.

Privately-owned country houses open to the public are far more than simply a matter of opening the doors. They depend upon their business enterprises for survival. The temptation at Bowood to dumb down or commercialise has been resisted, so that what is offered remains special and unspoiled. There is something for everyone to enjoy without detraction from the essential quality of experience which brings people back again and again.

The Open Days business makes a loss, and is unlikely to break even in the future; nevertheless, this vital element of engagement with the public, the *raison-d'être* of it all, is made possible despite multiple forms of taxation. At least for the time being, the loss can be offset by other, more profitable parts of the business which help to cover the enormous expenses of staffing, road and Listed building repairs, health and safety, insurance, and so on.

Two thirds of all visitors come with their families, almost certainly because of the good value for money and variety of things to do on a whole day out. Engaging the interest and enthusiasm of visiting children is a high priority, with Derry Hill School visits hosted in person by Lord Lansdowne.

The annual receptions for present and retired staff and their families, held in the summer and at Christmas since the 1970s, are welcome opportunities to bring Lansdowne family members together with those who work and live nearby. From 2013, Evensong has been held quarterly in the Bowood Chapel for all who would like to attend.

Those who work at Bowood, not forgetting the army of part-time seasonal staff, are part of an extended family whose loyalty and hard work, often under pressure, are tempered with good humour and pride in high standards and jobs well done. Bowood today provides employment for some 250 people, between 180 and 190 of whom are employed all the year round, and a number of whom gain work experience before going on to other jobs or further education.

An historic and present-day connection to Bowood is felt by many local people in Derry Hill and Studley village. Over time, as the village has expanded and the proportion of Estate employees and former employees has reduced, there has been a valuable influx of newcomers whose interests and experience are diverse; they and their children have helped to ensure that the village school, sports and social facilities and the shop remain viable and the future of a vibrant community is assured. The local and wider economies, of course, benefit substantially from Bowood's purchases of goods and services as well as visitor-expenditure.

Far more has happened at Bowood over the last 40 years or so than since the days of the 3rd Marquess in the 19th century when Bowood was at its zenith as a family estate. Things were very different then; the 3rd Marquess was wealthy and shrewd but, as can be seen from the archives, there were financial problems on his death in 1863 from which the Estate has perhaps never fully recovered.

Change and innovation have been vital to present-day success, along with nurturing and sharing the elements of Bowood that attract the public: a sense of history and of well-being that beautiful surroundings can give. Evolution is continual. The private gardens are now open to the public by special arrangement. Receptions are frequently held in the private rooms by Lord and Lady Lansdowne. New attractions are planned for each season.

The present Lord Lansdowne has never considered himself other than as a custodian. He is chief executive of the Bowood Enterprises, income from which is all ploughed back into the Estate. He has never taken a salary for what amounts to a highly-challenging life's work. He considers his occupation to be a labour of love as well as a duty. It gives him and Lady Lansdowne great pleasure to know how much Bowood and its facilities are enjoyed by so many people. Sometimes new enterprises work and sometimes they don't; battles of one kind or another occur too often for complacency. Nevertheless, a heritage business run by its caring owner has, so far, proved successful in preventing fragmentation and loss.

Looking to the future of Bowood, Lord Kerry, Lord Lansdowne's heir, will eventually inherit Bowood. He and his wife will decide how best to take the Estate forward in an exciting era of global proximity via the Internet and social media.